STREETWISE

BUSINESS
FORMS

STREETWISE

BUSINESS
FORMS

150 Professionally-
Designed Forms That
Will Bring Success
to Your Business

by Bob Adams

Adams Media Corporation
Holbrook, Massachusetts

Published by Adams Media Corporation
260 Center Street, Holbrook, MA 02343

ISBN: 1-58062-132-5

Printed in Canada.

J   I   H   G   F   E   D   C   B   A

Library of Congress Cataloging-in-Publication Data available from publisher.

This publication is designed to provide accurate and authoritative information with regard to the subject matter covered. It is sold with the understanding that the publisher is not engaged in rendering legal, accounting, or other professional advice. If legal advice or other expert assistance is required, the services of a competent professional person should be sought.
— From a *Declaration of Principles* jointly adopted by a Committee of the American Bar Association and a Committee of Publishers and Associations

Cover illustration by Eric Mueller.

This book is available at quantity discounts for bulk purchases.
For information, call 1-800-872-5627 (in Massachusetts, 781-767-8100).

Visit our exciting small business Web site: www.businesstown.com

Table of Contents

Contents

Introduction

Congratulations! You just purchased *STREETWISE Business Forms* that will save you, your small business, or your office time and money, and it will improve the image you project to your customers, suppliers, and employees. And you have a CD-ROM to customize and simplify productivity of your forms.

You can begin to reap the benefits of this book and CD-ROM immediately, by saving countless hours that would otherwise have been spent designing and assembling your own forms. And you may well find that the "payback period" on this book has been reached with your very first use. By photocopying a single batch of forms, your business will bypass the expenses, not only of design and production, but also of the costly delays that so often accompany jobs given to commercial printers.

However, this book is far more than a money-and time saver. *STREETWISE Business Forms* is an efficient management tool. The forms it contains will help you speed the collection of receivables, boost sales, track inventories, record expenses, organize workflow, evaluate job applicants, reduce phone costs, make credit decisions, evaluate payroll, prepare budgets, and much more.

Perhaps most importantly, this book has been designed to yield years of use. Until now, business form books have either been of the self-destruct type (pages ripped out to lie flat on the copier) or saddle-stitched (in which one pounded the book in an unsuccessful attempt to provide a level surface and undistorted copies). *STREETWISE Business Forms* features a perforated form. As an added benefit all the forms are on the attached CD-ROM and then are active where applicable i.e., the forms will add, subtract, multiply, and divide for you. The result? Crisp, straight copies without effort, frustration, or wear and tear.

If you want to find one of the forms from the book on the enclosed CD-ROM, simply insert the disk, click on Open a Master Document and follow the steps outlined at the bottom of the form you have chosen.

STREETWISE Business Forms is divided into 13 sections. Each section is packed with valuable forms that will contribute to the profitability and efficiency of your business.

Attracting Customers

Chapter 1

Forms for quotes, estimates, bids, and proposals

Whether your business is a one-person-house-painting service or a major engineering firm, your first meeting with a prospective customer is very important. Professional-looking forms such as the ones we have included in this chapter for *quotes, estimates, bids*, and *proposals*, go a long way toward projecting a professional image. A clean, well-organized quote implies professional, quality and efficient workmanship. It also implies that you are serious about your business, and that you will fulfill your obligations, and that you can be counted on to complete the work on time.

Remember that once you have left the customer, all you leave behind is the form outlining your quote. Leaving behind a professional-looking quote, estimate, bid, or proposal tells the customer your business is well-established and well-run. When the prospective customer sits down to evaluate your quote or estimate and those of your competitors, you can be assured that the professionally prepared quotes will have a competitive edge over ones scribbled on a piece of scrap paper, or on the back of an envelope.

Simply put, professional-looking forms for quotes, estimates, bids, and proposals build customer confidence and will help turn prospects into customers.

BID

Submitted by:

Date prepared: _____

Valid until: _____

Prepared for: _____

_____

_____

_____

_____

Cost details: _____

_____

Item/Description	Amount

Total Bid Price | $ - |

Comments/Specifications:

Price Valid Until

Prepared by: _____

ESTIMATE-1

From:

Date prepared: _____

Prepared for: _____
_____
_____
_____

Materials

Item/Description	Number	Cost per	Amount
			$ -
			$ -
			$ -
			$ -
			$ -
			$ -
			$ -

Material costs | $ - |

Labor

Item/Description	Number	Cost per	Amount
			$ -
			$ -
			$ -
			$ -
			$ -
			$ -
			$ -

Labor costs | $ - |

Total Estimated Costs | $ - |

Path on CD-ROM: Attracting Customers (01)→Estimate-1.xls

ESTIMATE-2

From:

Date prepared:

Prepared for:

Materials

Item/Description	Number	Cost per	Amount
			$ -
			$ -
			$ -
			$ -
			$ -
		Material costs	$ -

Labor

Item/Description	Number	Cost per	Amount
			$ -
			$ -
			$ -
			$ -
			$ -
		Labor costs	$ -

Comments

Total Estimated Costs $ -

Authorized signature

Submitted by:

Date prepared: _____

Valid until: _____

Prepared for: _____

_____

_____

_____

Specifications: _____

_____

_____

_____

_____

_____

_____

_____

_____

_____

_____

_____

_____

Schedule: _____

_____

Cost: _____

Terms: _____

Prepared by: _____

Path on CD-ROM: Attracting Customers(01)→Proposal.xls

QUOTATION

From:

Date prepared: _____

Valid until: _____

Quotation number: _____

Prepared for: _____

_____

_____

_____

_____

Item/Description	Number of units	Unit price	Amount
			$ -
			$ -
			$ -
			$ -
			$ -
			$ -
			$ -
			$ -
			$ -
			$ -
			$ -
			$ -
			$ -

Total $ -

Terms and conditions

Prepared by: _____

Sales Closers

Chapter 2

Order forms, work orders, receipts, and more

Neat, clean, and well-organized *order forms* and *work orders* insure that your customers get the exact products and services that they want, when they want them.

Professional order forms, properly prepared and processed, will also help avoid time-consuming and irritating follow-up phone calls to obtain more information. In addition, having an order form ready to be filled out can help close sales—just as estimating a price or suggesting a product can often persuade a hesitant prospect to go ahead with the purchase.

Order forms can also improve relations with customers and avoid uncertainties or disputes. If a customer orders five items but later only remembers ordering four, and if you can produce the order form showing the actual order placed, a difficult situation can be avoided.

Additionally, by giving the customer a copy of a professional-looking order form, you will appear more professional and be treated more professionally. A customer will have more confidence in your product or service, even before the product is delivered or before the work begins.

Receipts are particularly important in a cash business. By keeping copies of each receipt, and giving a receipt to every customer, a business owner can double-check the cash position and ascertain that no cash has disappeared unaccounted for. To ensure that customers ask for a receipt, many businesses post signs at the check-out point saying: "No returns or refunds without a receipt."

Receipts are important in non-cash businesses as well. As with order forms, professional-looking receipts help build customers' confidence and underscore the fact that they are dealing with a professionally-run business.

LAYAWAY RECORD

From: Date: _____
                                        Salesperson: _____

Sold to: _____
         _____
         _____
Telephone: _____

Item/Description	Price per	Quantity	Amount
			$ -
			$ -
			$ -
			$ -
			$ -
			$ -
			$ -
			$ -
			$ -
			$ -
			$ -
			$ -
			$ -
			$ -
			$ -
			$ -
			$ -
			$ -
			$ -
			$ -
			$ -
			$ -
		Subtotal	$ -
		Sales Tax	$ -
		Total Due	$ -
		Deposit	
		Balance	$ -

Pick-up date: _____

Delivery schedule: _____

ORDER BLANK

From: _____

Order date: _____
Number: _____
Salesperson: _____
Date: _____

Sold to: _____

Ship to: _____

Telephone: _____

Ship by: _____

Shipping date: _____

Quantity	Item/Description	Price per	Amount
			$ -
			$ -
			$ -
			$ -
			$ -
			$ -
			$ -
			$ -
			$ -
			$ -
			$ -
			$ -
			$ -
		Subtotal	$ -
		Sales tax	$ -
		Shipping	
		Total Due	$ -

Terms of Payment

Cash _____
On account #: _____
COD _____
Charge: _____
Other _____

Path on CD-ROM: Sales Closers (02)→Order Blank.xls

PHONE ORDER-1

From:

Number: _____

Account number: _____

Shipping instructions: _____

Date: _____

Sold to: _____

_____

_____

_____

_____

Ship to: _____

_____

_____

_____

_____

Quantity Ordered	Item/Description	No. shipped	No. backordered	Price per	Amount
					$ -
					$ -
					$ -
					$ -
					$ -
					$ -
					$ -
					$ -
					$ -
					$ -
					$ -
					$ -
					$ -
					$ -
					$ -
					$ -
					$ -
					$ -
					$ -
					$ -
					$ -
					$ -
				Subtotal	$ -
				Shipping	
				Total	$ -

Terms: _____

Salesperson _____

Path on CD-ROM: Sales Closers (02)→Phone Order-1.xls

PHONE ORDER-2

From: _____

Order date: _____
Number: _____
Account number: _____
Instructions: _____
Date: _____

Sold to:

Customer: _____
Attn: _____
Street: _____
City: _____
State/Zip: _____

Ship to: _____

Customer: _____
Attn: _____
Street: _____
City: _____
State/Zip: _____

Delivery date: _____
Shipping date: _____
Ship via: _____

No. ordered	Item/Description	No. shipped	Price per	Amount
				$ -
				$ -
				$ -
				$ -
				$ -
				$ -
				$ -
				$ -
				$ -
				$ -
				$ -
			Subtotal	$ -

Terms of Payment

Cash: _____
COD: _____
On account #: _____
Charge: _____
Other: _____

Total: $ -

Salesperson: _____

RECEIPT

From: Receipt number: _____
                                         Date: _____

Received from: _____   Amount due: [   ]
Amount: _____   This payment: [▓▓▓▓▓▓▓▓]
Signed: _____   Balance due: $ -

RECEIPT

From: Receipt number: _____
                                         Date: _____

Received from: _____   Amount due: [   ]
Amount: _____   This payment: [▓▓▓▓▓▓▓▓]
Signed: _____   Balance due: $ -

RECEIPT

From: Receipt number: _____
                                         Date: _____

Received from: _____   Amount due: [   ]
Amount: _____   This payment: [▓▓▓▓▓▓▓▓]
Signed: _____   Balance due: $ -

Path on CD-ROM: Sales Closers (02)→Receipt.xls

SPECIAL REQUEST

From:

Order date: _____

Date required: _____

Number: _____

Instructions: _____

_____

Sold to:

Customer: _____

Attn: _____

Street: _____

City: _____

State/Zip: _____

Telephone: _____

Method of payment: ☐ Cash   ☐ Charge

☐ COD   ☐ Other

Quantity	Item/Description	Unit price	Amount
			$ -
			$ -
			$ -
			$ -
			$ -
			$ -
			$ -
			$ -
			$ -
			$ -
			$ -
			$ -
			$ -
			$ -
			$ -
			$ -

Amount Due | $ - |

Salesperson: _____

WORK ORDER

From:

Date prepared: _____

Prepared for: _____

_____

_____

_____

_____

Materials

Item/Description	Number	Cost per	Amount
			$ -
			$ -
			$ -
			$ -
			$ -
			$ -
			$ -

Material Costs $ -

Labor

Item/Description	Number	Cost per	Amount
			$ -
			$ -
			$ -
			$ -
			$ -
			$ -
			$ -

Labor Costs $ -

Total Estimated Costs $ -

Customer Correspondence

Chapter 3

Forms that professionalize your image

Any time you communicate with a customer, you need to maintain a professional image. For jotting a quick note to a customer, the memo form is perfect. By using this form you will present a professional image without going to the time of typing up a formal letter with complete address and greeting on letterhead. Because of its informal yet professional appearance, a memo allows you to zero-in on the issue at hand and skip formalities.

Packing slips are important to show the exact quantity and nature of the products you delivered. By using packing slips, you place the burden on the customer to challenge the accuracy of your delivery at the time of receipt. Otherwise, a business has no exact proof of the items and quantities shipped. Packing slips also bring shipping errors to the surface quickly and allow you to resolve them before they become catastrophic problems.

Some companies have every packing slip initialed by the employee that picks and packs the shipment. This not only allows the firms to immediately identify the person who inaccurately picks or packs a shipment, but perhaps more importantly,

also encourages shipping room personnel to take extra care in their work.

Packing slips are essential when you do business with any other company, even if you are selling only a single product. Without packing slips, you will probably need to wait longer to have your invoices processed—and will occasionally be told that your shipment was never received.

Your business might use the *credit/debit memos* or *return authorization notices* only occasionally. However, the times that you have to use these forms (for example, when a bill is being disputed), might be a critical moment with an important customer—a time when a professional-looking form, resolving the problem with the issuance of credit or debit, could make a difference in keeping the customer.

The *"We Missed You"* form is important as well; it shows that you did your job and attempted to deliver your service or product on time, but that the customer was not there.

You can bolster your image by presenting yourself professionally every time you correspond with a customer. Since these forms frequently take even less time to write than a quick note, there is no reason not to appear professional in your correspondence!

AUTHORIZATION FOR RETURN

From:

Date: _____
Order number: _____
Order date: _____

Sold to: Return to:

_____   _____
_____   _____
_____   _____
_____   _____
_____   _____

Quantity	Item/Description	Unit price	Amount
			$ -
			$ -
			$ -
			$ -
			$ -
			$ -
			$ -
			$ -
			$ -
			$ -
			$ -
			$ -
			$ -
			$ -
			$ -

Reason for return: _____   Total | $ - |
_____
_____
_____

Approved by: _____

Date: _____

CREDIT NOTICE

From: _____

Date: _____
Date issued: _____
Customer number: _____
Order number: _____

Credit to: _____

Shipping address: _____
_____
_____
_____
_____

Dear Customer: We have adjusted your account to reflect the following transaction(s).

Items Returned _____   Date received: _____

Quantity	Item/Description	Price per	Amount	Explanation
			$ -	
			$ -	
			$ -	
			$ -	
			$ -	
			$ -	
			$ -	
			$ -	
			$ -	
			$ -	
			$ -	
			$ -	
			$ -	
			$ -	
			$ -	

Total Credit Adjustment $ -

Remarks: _____
_____
_____
_____

Approved by: _____

Date: _____

Path on CD-ROM: Customer Correspondence (03)→Credit Notice.xls

DEBIT NOTICE

From: Date: _____

                                         Date issued: _____

                                    Customer number: _____

                                        Order number: _____

Credit to: _____   Shipping address: _____

           _____   _____

           _____   _____

           _____   _____

           _____   _____

           _____   _____

Dear Customer: We have adjusted your account to reflect the following transaction(s).

Quantity	Item/Description	Price per	Amount	Explanation
			$ -	
			$ -	
			$ -	
			$ -	
			$ -	
			$ -	
			$ -	
			$ -	
			$ -	
			$ -	
			$ -	
			$ -	
			$ -	
			$ -	
			$ -	

                              Total Debit Adjustment $ -

Remarks: _____   Approved by: _____

         _____

         _____   Date: _____

         _____

Path on CD-ROM: Customer Correspondence (03)→Debit Notice.xls

PACKING SLIP

From:

Date: _____

Order number: _____

Invoice number: _____

Sold to:

Customer: _____

Attn: _____

Street: _____

City: _____

State/Zip: _____

Ship to:

Customer: _____

Attn: _____

Street: _____

City: _____

State/Zip: _____

Ship via: _____

No. ordered	Item/Description	No. shipped	Cartons	Total weight

Total shipped | 0 | 0 | 0 |

Packer: _____

REQUEST FOR SAMPLES

From: Date:

Sold to: _____

Customer _____

Title: _____

Street _____

City: _____

State/Zip: _____

Telephone: _____

Previous Customer _____   New Account _____

Account number: _____   Account number: _____

Quantity	Item/Description
0	Total Quantity

Shipping instructions: _____

Authorizing signature: _____

WE MISSED YOU

From: Date: _____

We were here on _____   at   _____
Please call us at: _____
between _____   and   _____ to arrange another visit.
Signed: _____

WE MISSED YOU

From: Date: _____

We were here on _____   at   _____
Please call us at: _____
between _____   and   _____ to arrange another visit.
Signed: _____

WE MISSED YOU

From: Date: _____

We were here on _____   at   _____
Please call us at: _____
between _____   and   _____ to arrange another visit.
Signed: _____

Path on CD-ROM: Customer Correspondence (03)→We Missed You.xls

Sales
Builders

Chapter 4

Forms that help increase your sales

Whether you have a hundred-person sales force or handle all of your customers personally, meticulous use of the enclosed forms can send your sales soaring! All small business owners or salespersons can increase their sales and earnings significantly by taking a small amount of time to maintain meticulous records on every qualified prospect and customer.

Every person or business who shows an interest in your product or service is a qualified lead. Every person who calls your business asking for a quote—or merely for information—is a qualified lead. Every person who wanders into your shop is a qualified lead. Any one of these people is much more likely to buy your product or service than someone you have not had contact with. By carefully following up on each lead, you can greatly increase your customer base without spending money for expensive advertising.

To follow up qualified leads, you need to ask prospective customers for their names, phone numbers, and addresses. You can use the *sales lead tracking sheet* to take information from a prospective customer who calls and inquires about your services or products. You can then follow-up by calling back the prospect in a few days to renew interest in your services or products. The *sales lead tracking sheet* is designed to enable you to make notes on several additional calls to a prospect. By using this sheet, you can keep track of when you last spoke with the prospect and what their level of interest and concerns were on your most recent call.

If you have a retail location, you can build up a large pool of qualified leads by simply putting the *mailing list* in a highly visible location with a small sign beside it. You can send multiple mailings, such as postcards, to people on this list, reminding them of your services or products. A stronger inducement would be to announce a sale or, better yet, to send a coupon for a discount on their next purchase.

Of course, one of the strongest uses of the mailing list form is to build repeat sales within your existing customer base. If your product is one that the same customer can use more than once, then you should send mailings frequently. It is much easier to sell the same customer again than to attract a new customer. Even if your business is one which deals primarily with one-shot sales, such as an aluminum siding contracting business, you still can benefit tremendously by careful use of a mailing list. For example, you can ask existing customers to refer their friends and relatives to you and announce a special limited-time offer.

Every salesperson needs to keep careful records of his and her phone calls and customer visits; we have included several forms for this purpose. In addition, self-employed and other small businesspeople can benefit by carefully building lists of qualified prospects and by aggressively following up on them.

For salespeople and sales managers, detailed records are vital. *Sales reports* show the amount of completed contacts from one day to the next. Sales reports show who is worthwhile to follow up, who is not, when a prospect should be followed up, and what their primary needs or concerns are.

We offer a large variety of sales reports so that you can choose the one best suited to your own purposes. Included are a *daily appointment log*, a *telephone call report*, a *daily call report*, a *salesperson's visit log*, and a *salesperson's daily record*.

Sales reps are best served by having all of their information organized on an account-by-account, as opposed to a day-by-day, basis. A salesperson should have one centralized record of every previous conversation with an account in front of him or her when an account is called. Again, we have included several forms to choose from: the *contact summary*, the *sales lead tracking sheet*, and the *proposal follow-up* all have room to summarize information from multiple contacts with a customer. A well-organized sales rep should rely primarily on these forms for keeping notes about prospects and customers, and should only use *daily call reports* and related forms to submit to sales managers.

As soon as the sales rep feels it would be worthwhile to call a prospect a second time, he or she should start using a form such as the *contact summary form*. This ensures all of the information on the client will be on one form without the sales rep needing to take extra time to copy if from other forms.

ADDRESS LIST

Page: _____

Date revised: _____

Name	Address	Zip code	Area code	Telephone

Path on CD-ROM: Sales Builders (04)→Address List.xls

CLIENT/PROSPECT CONTACT SUMMARY

Company: _____

Contact: _____

Street: _____

City/State/Zip: _____

Telephone: _____

Representative: _____

Product: _____

Date	Comment	When to call next?	Sale?

Path on CD-ROM: Sales Builders (04)→Client Prospect Contact Summary.xls

DAILY APPOINTMENT LOG

Date: _____

Client/Account	Service type	Scheduled visit	Begin time	End time	Next visit date	Comments

Name: _____

Location: _____

Path on CD-ROM: Sales Builders (04)→Daily Appointment Log.xls

DAILY CALL REPORT

Date: _____

Page: _____

Name: _____   Telephone: _____

Street: _____   Fax: _____

City/State./Zip: _____

Product line: _____   Territory: _____

Firm name/Location	Contact name/Title/Telephone	Result	Follow-up?	$ Sold

Comments: _____   Total Sales $ _____ -

_____

_____

Path on CD-ROM: Sales Builders (04)→Daily Call Report.xls

DISCOUNT WORKSHEET

Date: _____

Prepared by: _____

Item/Description	Retail price	Date valid from	Date valid to	Percent discount	Final unit price
					$ -
					$ -
					$ -
					$ -
					$ -
					$ -
					$ -
					$ -
					$ -
					$ -
					$ -
					$ -
					$ -
					$ -
					$ -
					$ -
					$ -
					$ -
					$ -
					$ -
					$ -
					$ -
					$ -
					$ -
					$ -
					$ -
					$ -
					$ -
					$ -
					$ -
					$ -
					$ -

MAILING LIST

Page: _____

Date revised: _____

Name	Address	Zip code	Customer no.	Date added	Mailing sent	Delete

Path on CD-ROM: Sales Builders (04)→Mailing List.xls

PROPOSAL FOLLOW-UP

Date: _____

Period: _____

Representative: _____

		Date last contacted	Proposal	Response	Follow-up
Company:					
Address:					
Telephone:					
Contact:					
Company:					
Address:					
Telephone:					
Contact:					
Company:					
Address:					
Telephone:					
Contact:					
Company:					
Address:					
Telephone:					
Contact:					
Company:					
Address:					
Telephone:					
Contact:					

Path on CD-ROM: Sales Builders (04)→Proposal Follow-Up.xls

SALES LEAD TRACKING SHEET

Name: _____

Street: _____

City: _____

State/Zip: _____

Telephone: _____

Contact person: _____

Product: _____

Date	Contents of call	Follow-up	Remarks

SALESPERSON DAILY RECORD

Date: _____

Page: _____

Salesperson: _____

Company name	Address/Telephone	Contact	Sold?	Comments

Contacts Made [_____] [_____] Total Sales

SALESPERSON VISIT LOG

Date: _____

Page: _____

Name: _____   Telephone: _____

Street: _____   Fax: _____

City/State/Zip: _____

Firm name/Location	Contact name/Title	Telephone	Result	$ Sold	Follow-up?

Comments: _____   Total Sales $ -

_____

_____

_____

Path on CD-ROM: Sales Builders (04)→Visit Log.xls

TELEPHONE CALL REPORT

Date from:

Date to:

Page:

Name: Telephone:

Street: Fax:

City/State./Zip:

Firm name/Location	Contact name/Title	Telephone	Result	$ Sold

Comments:

Total Sales $ -

TELEPHONE LOG REPORT

Month of: _____

Page number: _____

Date	Time	Caller	Department	Call to	Company/address	City	Area code	Telephone

Path on CD-ROM: Sales Builders (04)→Telephone Log Report.xls

Expense Controllers

Chapter 5

Forms that control and reduce costs

If only for basic tax purposes, every business must be able to show expense totals by category. And if your business is ever audited, the IRS or State Tax Examiner will expect you to be able to show instantly how you derived the total for any expense category. As far as the tax auditors are concerned, if you can't immediately document an expenditure then the expenditure never occurred.

For example, when one of my businesses was audited, the examiner, who knew nothing about my business, said that my phone expenses seemed excessive and that I would have to immediately provide him with a summary of all the phone bills that I had paid. Fortunately, I had a neat summary of all of my expenses by category prepared on a form similar to the *expense record form*. Next, the auditor demanded two specific original phone invoices (you absolutely must save every single invoice you pay). As if that weren't enough, he insisted that my business phone calls were personal calls! If I had maintained a *telephone log report* I would have had nothing to worry about; since I didn't, he disallowed some of my business phone calls as personal calls. I was completely at his mercy without a phone call record; he could conceivably have disallowed deduction of my entire phone bill!

For income tax purposes, you must record each expense by category, as soon as the expense is made, on a form such as the *expense record*. Then, at year-end, before filling out your income tax forms, you must summarize your expenses by category using a form such as the *profit and loss statement*. You will want to record phone calls on a telephone log report to show that they were business calls. Another area in which the IRS is particularly stringent is the deduction of car and truck expenses. The best procedure is to keep a complete daily log such as the *monthly expense report* showing exactly when you used a vehicle for business or pleasure.

Besides tax purposes, recording expenses is very important in managing your business. To control and reduce your expenses you must start by carefully logging and summarizing them by category—as in the profit and loss statement and the expense record. Then look for areas where you can cut costs. Remember, any time you can cut expenses without cutting sales you are adding directly to your profits. If you have a 10% profit margin, then a 10% reduction in costs would add as much profit as a 100% increase in sales!

When you look at your expense record and try to reduce future costs, think not only of which expenses you might be able to avoid in the future, but also which purchases you might be able to find at a less expensive source of supply. The *request for bid* form will expedite obtaining estimates from several different suppliers.

The use of a *formal purchase order* can be very important. Any company—no matter how small—that uses purchase orders is more likely to be extended credit than a firm that does not. Written purchase orders also give you complete control, without argument, over all specifications of products and services that you are buying. Without using written purchase orders, suppliers will frequently make minor substitutions or alterations in their products or deliveries that will make you unhappy.

Purchase orders allow you to shave expenses too. For example, by specifying the shipment method, you may save money. Many suppliers consider a 10 percent or 15 percent overrun on a custom-made product (such as packing cartons) to be perfectly acceptable. If you do not want to accept an overrun, say so on the purchase order.

The *purchase order record* is crucial because it helps you to project your future cash needs. If you find that you are spending more than you can afford, then hold off buying more goods—or ask your suppliers for extended payment terms.

The *remittance form* is more important than you might think. You can save time by paying several bills from one supplier at one time (remember, time is money). If you do not carefully identify which invoices you are paying, you can easily burn up many hours in discussions with accounts receivable departments. The use of the remittance form can help avoid confusion by showing a supplier exactly which bills you are paying at one time.

Salespeople often seem to expect larger paychecks than they earn. One reason is that they tend to forget about tax withholdings. In any event, you can reduce the chance of disagreement with a salesperson over commissions by using a well-organized form such as the *commission summary* or *the salesperson's summary*.

Remember, time spent carefully recording expenses will not only save hours later, but can also help reduce tax bills and help you decide in which areas of your business you can trim expenses.

BID COMPARISON WORKSHEET

Description of project: _____
_____
_____
_____

Bid #1

Company name: _____

Estimate total: _____

Comments: _____
_____
_____

Bid #2

Company name: _____

Estimate total: _____

Comments: _____
_____
_____

Bid #3

Company name: _____

Estimate total: _____

Comments: _____
_____
_____

Recommendation for vendor:
_____
_____
_____
_____

COMMISSION SUMMARY

Period from: _____
Period to: _____
Salesperson: _____
Territory: _____

Date	Order number	Client	Extended	Commission percentage	Amount
					$ -
					$ -
					$ -
					$ -
					$ -
					$ -
					$ -
					$ -
					$ -
					$ -
					$ -
					$ -
					$ -
					$ -
					$ -
					$ -
					$ -
					$ -
					$ -
					$ -
					$ -
					$ -
					$ -
					$ -

Total Invoiced $ _____ -

Gross Commission Earned $ _____ -
Less Advance
Other Deductions

Date paid: _____

Amount Payable $ _____ -

EXPENSE RECORD

Month of: _____

Page number: _____

Date	Amount of Expense	Budget Category																			

Path on CD-ROM: Expense Controllers (05)→Expense Record.xls

MONTHLY EXPENSE RECORD

Month of: _____

Name: _____

Day	Budget Category																					

MONTHLY EXPENSE REPORT

From: _____

To: _____

Name: _____

Position: _____

Day	Travel	Auto	Meals	Lodging	Entertainment	Other	Daily Totals
1							$ -
2							$ -
3							$ -
4							$ -
5							$ -
6							$ -
7							$ -
8							$ -
9							$ -
10							$ -
11							$ -
12							$ -
13							$ -
14							$ -
15							$ -
16							$ -
17							$ -
18							$ -
19							$ -
20							$ -
21							$ -
22							$ -
23							$ -
24							$ -
25							$ -
26							$ -
27							$ -
28							$ -
29							$ -
30							$ -
31							$ -

Path on CD-ROM: Expense Controllers (05)→Monthly Expense Report.xls

PROFIT AND LOSS STATEMENT

Year: _____

INCOME

Gross sales:	
Less returns:	
Less bad debts:	
Interest, rent, royalty income:	
Total Income:	$ -

EXPENSES

Cost of goods sold:	
Direct payroll:	
Indirect payroll:	
Taxes, other than income tax:	
Sales expenses:	
Shipping, postage:	
Advertising, promotion:	
Office expenses:	
Travel, entertainment:	
Phone:	
Other utilities:	
Auto/truck:	
Insurance:	
Professional fees:	
Rent:	
Interest on loans:	
Other:	

Total Expenses before Tax:	$ -
Total Income:	$ -
Net Income:	$ -
Income Tax:	
Net Income after Tax:	$ -

Path on CD-ROM: Expense Controllers (05)→Profit and Loss Statement.xls

PURCHASE ORDER RECORD

Date from: _____

Date to: _____

Page: _____

P.O. number	Date	Issued to	Item/Description	Due	Total Amount

Sheet Total $ -

Path on CD-ROM: Expense Controllers (05)→Purchase Order Record.xls

PURCHASE ORDER-1

From:

Date: _____

Order number: _____

Date wanted: _____

Terms: _____

To: _____

Ship via: _____

_____

_____

_____

Our Purchase Order Number must appear on all invoices, cases, packing lists and correspondence.

Quantity	Item/Description	Price per	Amount
			$ -
			$ -
			$ -
			$ -
			$ -
			$ -
			$ -
			$ -
			$ -
			$ -
			$ -
			$ -
			$ -
			$ -
			$ -
			$ -
			$ -
			$ -
			$ -
			$ -
			$ -
			$ -

Total Cost $ -

Authorized signature: _____

PURCHASE ORDER-2

From: Date:

                                         Order number:

                                         | Our Purchase Order Number must appear on all invoices, cases, packing lists and correspondence. |

To: Date wanted:

                                         Terms:

                                         Ship via:

Quantity	Item/Description	Price per	Amount
			$ -
			$ -
			$ -
			$ -
			$ -
			$ -
			$ -
			$ -
			$ -
			$ -
			$ -
			$ -
			$ -
			$ -
			$ -
			$ -
			$ -
			$ -
			$ -
			$ -
			$ -
			$ -
			$ -

Total Cost | $ - |

Authorized signature: _____

REMITTANCE

Date: _____

Your Invoice #			Deductions			
Invoice #	Date	Amount	Date	Explanation	Amount	Discount
						$ -
						$ -
						$ -
						$ -
						$ -
						$ -
						$ -
						$ -
						$ -
						$ -
						$ -
						$ -
						$ -
						$ -
						$ -
						$ -
						$ -
						$ -
						$ -
						$ -
						$ -
						$ -
						$ -
						$ -
						$ -
						$ -
						$ -

Amount Paid $ -

REQUEST FOR BID

From:

Date: _____

Valid until: _____

Quantity	Item/Description	Price per	Amount
			$ -
			$ -
			$ -
			$ -
			$ -
			$ -
			$ -
			$ -
			$ -
			$ -
			$ -
			$ -
			$ -
			$ -
			$ -
			$ -
			$ -
			$ -
			$ -
			$ -
			$ -
			$ -
			$ -
			$ -

Delivery and shipping requirements:	Total Due $ -

Signed: _____

SALESPERSON'S SUMMARY

Date from: _____

Date to: _____

Name: _____

Date	Order number	Client	Extended	Commission percentage	Commission amount
					$ -
					$ -
					$ -
					$ -
					$ -
					$ -
					$ -
					$ -
					$ -
					$ -
					$ -
					$ -
					$ -
					$ -
					$ -
					$ -
					$ -
					$ -
					$ -
					$ -
					$ -
					$ -
					$ -
					$ -

Total Invoiced Sales $ -

Gross Commission Earned $ -

Less Advances [   ]

Date paid: _____

Commission Due $ -

TELEPHONE LOG REPORT

Month of: _____

Page number: _____

Date	Time	Caller	Department	Call to	Company/address	City	Area code	Telephone

Path on CD-ROM: Expense Controllers (05)→Telephone Log Report.xls

TRIP EXPENSE RECORD

Name: _____

Trip: _____

Item								Total	
Airfare								$	-
Car rental, taxi								$	-
Auto Mileage								$	-
Parking/tolls								$	-
Lodging								$	-
Telephone								$	-
Misc. exp.								$	-
Total	$ -	$ -	$ -	$ -	$ -	$ -	$ -		$ -
Breakfast								$	-
Lunch								$	-
Dinner								$	-
Entertainment								$	-
Total	$ -	$ -	$ -	$ -	$ -	$ -	$ -		$ -

Entertainment

Date	Who	Place	Business	Amount

Other Expenses

Date	Description	Amount

Account Distribution

Entity ID	Acct	Sub Acct	Amount	
			$	-
			$	-
		TOTAL	$	-

Employee Signature _____   Approved By: _____

VOUCHER / ACCOUNTS PAYABLE

Date: _____

Voucher number: _____

Payable to:		Date	Account number	Extended
Approved by:				
Date				
Check number:				
Comments:				
		Net Payable	$	-

Payable to:		Date	Account number	Extended
Approved by:				
Date				
Check number:				
Comments:				
		Net Payable	$	-

Payable to:		Date	Account number	Extended
Approved by:				
Date				
Check number:				
Comments:				
		Net Payable	$	-

Path on CD-ROM: Expense Controllers (05)→Voucher Accounts Payable.xls

Inventory
Managers

Chapter 6

Forms that control your inventory

The importance of inventory management is often overlooked by small businesses. Nevertheless, it is impossible to manage your inventory too closely.

Many small businesspeople underestimate the cost of carrying inventory and the cost of stocking out. Too much inventory will bloat your costs, eat up your cash, and kill your growth prospects! But inventory stock-outs will not only kill potential sales, but can also lose customers permanently.

First, remember that the money you have invested in inventory, costs you more than the interest on the inventory loan and costs more money than the money could earn in the bank. Why? The money you have tied up in inventory could be used to expand your business, where it could probably earn you a lot more money than in the bank! Then there is the cost of insuring the inventory, the cost of shipping it in, and inventory taxes. Another very important cost is the cost of storing the inventory. You could say storage doesn't cost you anything because you don't rent a separate building for it? Think again. If you have a retail store and a storeroom at the same location, the storage cost might be the same as the additional revenue you could gain by enlarging your retail area into the storeroom area. Even if you do not have a retail store, storage space always has other uses such as accommodating a larger work area or a more efficient shipping room.

Another cost in carrying inventory is the risk of damage, and, more importantly, the risk of obsolescence. If your inventory is outdated by a newer version and you can't return it, you could take a major loss.

Of course, at any time you are out of stock of an item you risk losing a sale. You can minimize this risk by using two forms. The first is the *out of stock notice*. By sending this form to a customer (or distributing it in the store) you can keep the customer's order and tell them when you will expect to receive the item. Another form that will help is the *backorder record*. Here you need to carefully record all orders for items that are out of stock. This way you can keep track of how many and which out of stock items you need and press suppliers accordingly. However, the more you stock out, the greater the risk of losing customers. (Our firm switched suppliers of office supplies primarily because the previous vendor stocked out so frequently.)

The *inventory report* is the basic form for controlling inventory. By keeping inventory records you will know exactly what is in stock and how fast it is selling (by looking at the previous inventory reports). Then you can project when you should reorder to minimize excess inventory on hand and also minimize the chance of stocking out. We have included several inventory report forms; one of the basic differences between them is that some allow you to trace all deliveries and shipments on an individual item, whereas others are designed for recording a physical count of many different items on one form.

Daily shipping records are useful because they allow you to tell inquiring customers when to expect their orders. They can also help substantiate claims that items were shipped by you. However, a signature that the goods were received is the only way to truly substantiate that goods were delivered, not just shipped.

AUTHORIZATION TO DESTROY INVENTORY

Number: _____   Date: _____

Reason for Request to Destroy Inventory:

_____

_____

_____

Item#	Description	Quantity

Prepared by: _____   Date: _____

Approved by: _____   Date: _____

Copy to Inventory Control, Accounting, Warehouse Manager and Files.

Path on CD-ROM: Inventory Managers (06)→Authorization to Destroy Inventory.xls

BACKORDER RECORD

Date from: _____

Date to: _____

Item/Description	Number ordered	Number backordered	Date ordered from supplier	Date due	Date received

Path on CD-ROM: Inventory Managers (06)→Backorder Record.xls

INVENTORY CHANGES

Item/Description: _____

Sheet number: _____

ORDERED				RECEIVED				SOLD				
Date	PO #	Quantity	Due	Date	PO #	Quantity	Date	Invoice #	Amount sold	Net stock		
										○		
										○		
										○		
										○		
										○		
										○		
										○		
										○		
										○		
										○		
										○		
										○		
										○		
										○		
										○		
										○		
										○		
										○		

Path on CD-ROM: Inventory Managers (06)→Inventory Changes.xls

INVENTORY REPORT-1

Date: _____
To: _____
Name: _____
Position: _____

	Quantity	Unit	Item/Description	Unit price	Total
1					$ -
2					$ -
3					$ -
4					$ -
5					$ -
6					$ -
7					$ -
8					$ -
9					$ -
10					$ -
11					$ -
12					$ -
13					$ -
14					$ -
15					$ -
16					$ -
17					$ -
18					$ -
19					$ -
20					$ -
21					$ -
22					$ -
23					$ -
24					$ -
25					$ -

Total $ -

Prepared by: _____

_____
_____
_____
_____

INVENTORY REPORT-2

Date from: _____

Date to: _____

Date	Description	P.O. #	Cost per	Amount	Receiver	Shipped		Net Stock
						Order #	Quantity	
								○
								○
								○
								○
								○
								○
								○
								○
								○
								○
								○
								○
								○
								○
								○
								○
								○
								○
								○
								○

Path on CD-ROM: Inventory Managers (06)→Inventory Report-2.xls

MERCHANDISE EXCHANGE

Date: _____

From: _____

Address: _____

_____

Telephone: _____

Quantity	Invoice/Order number	Item/Description	Price per	Total
				$ -
				$ -
				$ -
				$ -
				$ -
				$ -
				$ -
				$ -
				$ -
				$ -
				$ -
				$ -
				$ -
				$ -
				$ -
				$ -
				$ -
				$ -
				$ -
				$ -
				$ -
				$ -
				$ -
				$ -

Total return   0 $ -

Quantity   Amount

Return for exchange: _____

_____

_____

Path on CD-ROM: Inventory Managers (06)→Merchandise Exchange.xls

MERCHANDISE RETURN

Date: _____

From: _____

Address: _____

_____

Telephone: _____

Quantity	Invoice/Order number	Item/Description	Price per	Total
				$ -
				$ -
				$ -
				$ -
				$ -
				$ -
				$ -
				$ -
				$ -
				$ -
				$ -
				$ -
				$ -
				$ -
				$ -
				$ -
				$ -
				$ -
				$ -
				$ -
				$ -
				$ -

Credit as:

Exchange: _____

Credit: _____

Cash: _____

Check #: _____

Charge: _____

Total return | 0 | $ - |

Quantity   Amount

Reason for return: _____

_____

OUT-OF-STOCK NOTICE

From:

Date: _____

Order number: _____

Order date: _____

We cannot fill your order at this time because the items listed are temporarily out of stock.
We apologize for the inconvenience.

Item/Description	Quantity	Estimated shipping date

RECEIVING SLIP

From: Date: _____

                                  Order/Invoice number: _____

Delivered to: _____

             _____

             _____

             _____

             _____

The following has been received in good order:

Quantity	Item/Description

                    Received by: _____

DAILY SHIPPING RECORD

Date: _____

Page: _____

Customer	Invoice number	Item/Description	Shipping address	Carrier	Zone	Cartons	Weight	Shipper

Path on CD-ROM: Inventory Managers (06)→Shipment Record.xls

Cash-Flow Maximizers

Professional invoices, statements, and cash records

Simply by issuing professional-looking invoices and statements, a small business will have its bills paid sooner. In fact, it may very well avoid the collection problems caused by unprofessional-looking invoices. This is especially true when dealing with other businesspeople, but it is also true when billing customers. Because professional-looking invoices are critical for all businesses, we have included several *invoice* forms from which to choose.

In one of my first businesses, I presented a client with an invoice I had produced quickly on a typewriter ten minutes before our scheduled meeting. His response: "What's this thing?" He may well have known it was an invoice, but he was definitely appalled at its unprofessional appearance. He did pay the bill—but if I had mailed him the invoice instead of showing up for payment in person, I might not have been so lucky. Even if I had "only "had to wait an extra week or two for payment, the point still stands—an invoice says a lot about the company that issues it, and about the likelihood of prompt payment.

Some businesses prefer to pay by *statements*, especially when you make more than one sale to them in a single month. Statements are sent in addition to, not instead of, invoices. By taking extra time to send statements in addition to invoices you can often speed payment and avoid follow-up phone calls.

Many businesses and consumers simply do not bother to pay their bills until they are reminded several times. In the following section on Bad Debt Collectors you'll find a variety of forms with which to collect old bills. However, the first step is to keep carefully organized records of money due to you on the *invoice record form*.

The best way to avoid billing problems and to speed cash flow is to get paid in advance. By using the *pro forma invoice* you can ask for payment in advance in a professional manner. This way, the customer has a copy of the invoice before he or she pays the bill, even though the service or goods have yet to be delivered.

The *bank deposit record* allows you to double-check payments from customers. If your customer insists that he or she paid a bill but you did not mark it as paid on your invoice record, you can double-check your bank deposit record. As your business grows, you will be surprised how often this situation will occur.

The other forms in this section help you control the flow of cash. If you are in a cash business, you must always be on your guard to track your cash trail as carefully as possible.

Remember, all firms and consumers expect professional-looking bills from any business, no matter how small. If you want to get paid and get paid on time for your services or products, be sure to use professional-looking invoices and statements.

BANK DEPOSIT RECORD-1

Date: _____

Page number: _____

CHECKS

	Name	Amount
1		
2		
3		
4		
5		
6		
7		
8		
9		
10		
11		
12		
13		
14		
15		
16		
17		
18		
19		
20		
21		

CHECKS

	Name	Amount
22		
23		
24		
25		
26		
27		
28		
29		
30		
31		
32		
33		
34		
35		
36		
37		
38		
39		
40		
41		
42		

TRAVELLER'S CHECKS

Name	Amount

CASH

	Amount
Cash	

Total Checks	$ -
Total Traveler's Checks	$ -
Cash	$ -
Total Deposit	$ -
Account no.:	

BANK DEPOSIT RECORD-2

Date: _____

Page number: _____

CHECKS		
	Name	Amount
1		
2		
3		
4		
5		
6		
7		
8		
9		
10		
11		
12		
13		
14		
15		
16		
17		
18		
19		
20		
21		
22		
23		
24		
25		
26		
27		

Total $ -

TRAVELLER'S CHECKS		
	Name	Amount

Total $ -

CASH		
	Name	Amount

Total $ -

Total Checks $ -

Total Traveler's Checks $ -

Cash $ -

Total Deposit $ -

Account no.: _____

Remarks

_____

_____

CASH DISBURSEMENT RECORD

Date from: _____

Date to: _____

Prepared by: _____

Checked by: _____

Date	Cash paid to	For item/description	Disbursed by	Account charged	Amount paid

Path on CD-ROM: Cash-Flow Maximizers (07)→Cash Disbursement Record.xls

CASHIER'S TILL RECORD

From:

Date: _____

Name: _____

Amount in till at start of day: [   ]

Item	Begin	End
Pennies		
Nickels		
Dimes		
Quarters		
Halves		
Dollars		
Fives		
Tens		
Twenties		
Fifties		
Hundreds		
Checks/Other		

Total | $ - | $ - |

Cashier Signature: _____

DAILY CASH RECORD

Date: _____

Page number: _____

CASH RECEIVED FROM		
	Name	Amount
1		
2		
3		
4		
5		
6		
7		
8		
9		
10		
11		
12		
13		
14		
15		
16		
17		
18		
19		
20		
21		
22		
23		
24		
25		
26		
27		

CASH PAID OUT		
	Name	Amount
1		
2		
3		
4		
5		
6		
7		
8		
9		
10		

Total $ -

Total Receipts $ -

Total Receipts $ -

Less Monies Paid Out $ -

Balance $ -

Remarks:

_____

INVOICE FOR WORK PERFORMED

Send Payment to:

Prepared by: _____

Date: _____

Materials

Date	Item/Description	Quantity	Unit price	Amount
				$ -
				$ -
				$ -
				$ -
				$ -
				$ -

Total | $ - |

Labor

Date	Item/Description	Quantity	Unit price	Amount
				$ -
				$ -
				$ -
				$ -
				$ -
				$ -

Total | $ - |

Travel and Miscellaneous Expenses

Total Invoice

Date	Description	Amount		Item	Amount
				Materials:	$ -
				Labor:	$ -
				Travel/Misc:	$ -
				Other:	

Total | $ - |

Total due | $ - |

INVOICE RECORD

Month of: _____

Page number: _____

Invoice number	Invoice date	Invoice amount	Company	Item/Description	Date paid	Check number

Path on CD-ROM: Cash-Flow Maximizers (07)→Invoice Record.xls

INVOICE-1

Send payment to:

> Please pay from this invoice;
> no statement will be issued.

Sold to: _____   Ship to: _____
         _____   _____
         _____   _____
         _____   _____
         _____   _____

Invoice no.: _____
Account no.: _____   Please indicate invoice number
Order no.: _____   in all communications
Salesperson: _____   regarding this invoice.
Date: _____

No. ordered	No. shipped	Item/Description	Unit price	Amount
				$ -
				$ -
				$ -
				$ -
				$ -
				$ -
				$ -
				$ -
				$ -
				$ -
				$ -
			Subtotal	$ -
			Sales tax	$ -
			Shipping/handling	
			Amount due	$ -

Thank you for your order

Path on CD-ROM: Cash-Flow Maximizers (07)→Invoice-1.xls

INVOICE-2

Send payment to:

Please pay from this invoice;
no statement will be issued.

Sold to: _____   Ship to: _____
_____   _____
_____   _____
_____   _____
_____   _____

Invoice no.: _____   Salesperson: _____
Order no.: _____   Date: _____
Account no.: _____

Please indicate invoice number in all
communications regarding this invoice.

No. ordered	No. shipped	Item/Description	Unit price	Amount
				$ -
				$ -
				$ -
				$ -
				$ -
				$ -
				$ -
				$ -
				$ -
				$ -
				$ -
				$ -
			Subtotal	$ -
			Sales tax	$ -
			Shipping/handling	
			Amount due	$ -

Thank you for your order

INVOICE-3

Send payment to:

Please pay from this invoice;
no statement will be issued.

Invoice no.: _____   Date: _____

Customer name: _____   Order no.: _____
Company: _____   Salesperson: _____
Street: _____   Shipped by: _____
City: _____
State/Zip: _____
Telephone: _____

No. ordered	No. shipped	Item/Description	Unit price	Amount
				$ -
				$ -
				$ -
				$ -
				$ -
				$ -
				$ -
				$ -
				$ -
				$ -
				$ -
				$ -
				$ -
				$ -
				$ -
				$ -
				$ -
				$ -
			Subtotal	$ -
			Sales tax	$ -
			Shipping/handling	
			Amount due	$ -

Thank you for your order

INVOICE-4

Send payment to:

Please pay from this invoice;
no statement will be issued.

Sold to:

Ship to:

Invoice no.: _____	
Account no.: _____	Please indicate invoice number
Order no.: _____	in all communications
Salesperson: _____	regarding this invoice.
Date: _____	

No. ordered	No. shipped	Item/Description	Unit price	Amount
				$ -
				$ -
				$ -
				$ -
				$ -
				$ -
				$ -
				$ -
				$ -
				$ -

Subtotal	$ -
Sales tax	$ -
Shipping/handling	
Amount due	$ -

Thank you for your order!

PETTY CASH LEDGER-1

From:

Date from: _____

Date to: _____

Prepared by: _____

Checked by: _____

Date	Payment number	Cash to	Amount paid	Cash added	Balance
		Balance on Hand			
					$ -
					$ -
					$ -
					$ -
					$ -
					$ -
					$ -
					$ -
					$ -
					$ -
					$ -
					$ -
					$ -
					$ -
					$ -
					$ -
					$ -
					$ -
					$ -
					$ -
					$ -
					$ -
					$ -
					$ -
					$ -
					$ -

Totals $ - $ -

Paid   Added

Balance forwarded $ -

PETTY CASH -2

Date: _____   For: _____

Amount: _____   _____

Approval: _____   _____

Account: _____   _____

Number: _____   _____

Received by: _____

PETTY CASH -2

Date: _____   For: _____

Amount: _____   _____

Approval: _____   _____

Account: _____   _____

Number: _____   _____

Received by: _____

PETTY CASH -2

Date: _____   For: _____

Amount: _____   _____

Approval: _____   _____

Account: _____   _____

Number: _____   _____

Received by: _____

Path on CD-ROM: Cash-Flow Maximizers (07)→Petty Cash Ledger-2.xls

PRO FORMA INVOICE

Send payment to:

	Please pay from this invoice; no statement will be issued.

Sold to: _____

_____

_____

_____

Ship to: _____

_____

_____

_____

Invoice no.: _____

Account no.: _____

Order no.: _____

Salesperson: _____

Date: _____

Please indicate invoice number in all communications regarding this invoice.

No. ordered	Item/Description	Unit price	Amount
			$ -
			$ -
			$ -
			$ -
			$ -
			$ -
			$ -
			$ -
			$ -
			$ -
			$ -
			$ -
			$ -
			$ -
			$ -
			$ -
			$ -
		Subtotal	$ -
		Sales tax	$ -
		Shipping/handling	
		Amount due	$ -

Thank you for your order

Path on CD-ROM: Cash-Flow Maximizers (07)→Pro-Forma Invoice.xls

STATEMENT

From: Date: _____

                                         Account no.: _____

To:

_____

_____

_____

_____

Date	Invoice number	Item/Description	Amount
		Balance forward	
		Payment -- THANK YOU!	

Please pay this amount: [   ]

VOUCHER/PETTY CASH

Date: _____

Voucher no.: _____

Description of use	Amount
Total	$ -

Account no.: _____

Approved by: _____

VOUCHER/PETTY CASH

Date: _____

Voucher no.: _____

Description of use	Amount
Total	$ -

Account no.: _____

Approved by: _____

VOUCHER/PETTY CASH

Date: _____

Voucher no.: _____

Description of use	Amount
Total	$ -

Account no.: _____

Approved by: _____

Path on CD-ROM: Cash-Flow Maximizers (07)→Voucher.xls

CASHIER'S VOUCHER

Voucher number: _____

Date: _____

Item/Description: _____   Paid to: _____

Requested by: _____

Approved by: _____   Amount: _____

CASHIER'S VOUCHER

Voucher number: _____

Date: _____

Item/Description: _____   Paid to: _____

Requested by: _____

Approved by: _____   Amount: _____

CASHIER'S VOUCHER

Voucher number: _____

Date: _____

Item/Description: _____   Paid to: _____

Requested by: _____

Approved by: _____   Amount: _____

Path on CD-ROM: Cash-Flow Maximizers (07)→Voucher Petty Cash.xls

Bad Debt Collectors

Forms that turn bad debts into cash

Some small businesses have bad debt running as high as 10 percent of sales, while other businesses keep it under 1 percent. By rigorously using the forms in this section you can keep your bad debt to an absolute minimum. Furthermore, you can use these forms to get your bills paid quickly and thereby increase the amount of cash you have on hand.

Most customers will eventually pay their bills. Some customers, as a matter of course, pay their bills extremely late—and a few simply don't have enough money on hand to keep up with all their bills. You should avoid extending credit to these bad credit risks. To do this, simply have accounts apply for credit by filling out an *application for credit*, then take the time to check their references. If their credit is poor, insist that they pay in advance. If their credit is questionable and you are unsure about extending credit, ask for partial payment and issue a receipt from the Sales Closers section of this book.

If you do decide to allow a customer to buy on credit, set up a credit limit and stick to it! Use the *credit record* to see that the customer is keeping current on their bills and that their total amount of credit is within your pre-assigned limit. Review each account regularly, and if an account is paying their bills more slowly than you would like, either cancel or reduce their credit line.

For all invoices and accounts that are overdue, you should promptly and regularly send out a *past due notice*. It is important to send these out at regular intervals to show the account that you are aware of the delay in payment and that you are serious about collecting it. Send out past due notices at least once a month.

Most overdue accounts will pay in full after receiving an overdue notice or two, but some always wait for a phone call. The *collection report* should be used to keep notes on calling overdue accounts. An alternative form to use is the contact summary form in the Sales Builders section of this book. Another alternative is to use the credit record form for recording overdue notices sent and overdue calls made. This form can also be used instead of the invoice record for recording sales to customers. Whichever forms you use, keep them in a safe place and keep them well-organized. Ideally, you should keep photocopies of all accounts receivable records in another location as well.

The *accounts receivable aging chart* is useful for showing the volume and age of your overdue accounts at the moment. It is also helpful in determining which overdue accounts to pursue first. In addition, this chart can help you project when you will be receiving payments from customers (for planning future cash flows as discussed later in the book).

Finally, the *returned check notification* form will make a strong impression on anyone who has written you a bad check. And if you haven't seen a bad check yet, you haven't been in business very long!

You have expended an enormous amount of time and money producing your goods and services, so be sure to go the extra distance to get paid for your work. Use these forms to collect every penny that you deserve!

ACCOUNT RECORD

Account no.: _____

Account name: _____

Page: _____

Date	Item/Description	Charge	Credit	Balance
				$ -

Path on CD-ROM: Bad Debt Collectors (08)→ Account Record.xls

ACCOUNTS RECEIVABLE AGING CHART

Date from: _____

Date to: _____

Customer	Invoice date	Invoice number	Item description	Current	30-60 days	60-90 days	90 days or more	Total
								$ -
								$ -
								$ -
								$ -
								$ -
								$ -
								$ -
								$ -
								$ -
								$ -
								$ -
								$ -
								$ -
								$ -
								$ -
								$ -
								$ -
								$ -
Total				$ -	$ -	$ -	$ -	$ -

APPLICATION FOR CREDIT

Please complete all sections, including account numbers and income sources. Alimony, child support payments, and public aid need not be included if you do not wish them to be considered as supporting your application for credit.

Name: _____	Address: _____
_____	_____
	_____
Telephone: _____	City/State/Zip: _____
_____	
	Length of time
	at this address: _____

Previous address: _____	City/State/Zip: _____
_____	
_____	_____

Current employer: _____	Address: _____
Period employed: _____	_____
Supervisor: _____	_____
Telephone: _____	City/State/Zip: _____
Position: _____	Yearly salary: _____

Previous employer: _____	Address: _____
Period employed: _____	_____
Supervisor: _____	_____
Telephone: _____	City/State/Zip: _____
Position: _____	Yearly salary: _____

Bank reference _____	Checking: _____
(Account numbers) _____	Savings: _____
_____	Name of bank: _____
	Other income: _____

Other credit references: (include daytime telephone numbers)

1 _____

2 _____

3 _____

COLLECTION REPORT

Company name: _____

Telephone number: _____

Address: _____

_____

_____

_____

1. Date: _____ Contact: _____ Invoice no. _____

Results: _____

Amount: _____

2. Date: _____ Contact: _____ Invoice no. _____

Results: _____

Amount: _____

3. Date: _____ Contact: _____ Invoice no. _____

Results: _____

Amount: _____

4. Date: _____ Contact: _____ Invoice no. _____

Results: _____

Amount: _____

5. Date: _____ Contact: _____ Invoice no. _____

Results: _____

Amount: _____

6. Date: _____ Contact: _____ Invoice no. _____

Results: _____

Amount: _____

7. Date: _____ Contact: _____ Invoice no. _____

Results: _____

Amount: _____

8. Date: _____ Contact: _____ Invoice no. _____

Results: _____

Amount: _____

Path on CD-ROM: Bad Debt Collectors (08)→Collection Report.xls

CREDIT RECORD

Date: _____
Credit line: [_____|_____]

Name: _____

Account no.: _____

Home address: _____

_____

Home telephone: _____

Business address: _____

_____

Business telephone: _____

Order number	Payment due		Payment received		Balance	First notice	Second notice
	Amount	Date	Amount	Date			
					$ -		
					$ -		
					$ -		
					$ -		
					$ -		
					$ -		
					$ -		
					$ -		
					$ -		
					$ -		
					$ -		
					$ -		
					$ -		
					$ -		
					$ -		
					$ -		
					$ -		
					$ -		
					$ -		

1st overdue call:	
2nd overdue call:	
3rd overdue call:	

Path on CD-ROM: Bad Debt Collectors (08)→Credit Record.xls

PAST DUE NOTICE

Date: _____

Account no.: _____

Your account is past due. Please remit the amount specified below.

Invoice number	Item/Description	Amount	Payment due

Payment due $ _____ -

RETURNED CHECK NOTIFICATION

From:

Date prepared: _____

Subject: _____

Customer: _____

_____

Address: _____

_____

_____

City/State/Zip: _____

_____

Telephone: _____

Your check no.: _____

Amount: _____

Date of check: _____

Bank: _____

We hold your check returned unpaid from your bank.

Please send new payment immediately.

Signed: _____

Time Planners

Chapter 9

Forms that turn time into money

In business, time is money! Every minute of every business day is time that could be spent making money. Unfortunately, some time must be spent in non-revenue-related tasks such as paying bills, paying taxes, cleaning the office, etcetera. Such tasks reduce the amount of time that can be spent on revenue-producing work making such time even more precious.

By using the *daily, weekly, monthly,* and *yearly organizers* you can prioritize your work, use your time more effectively, and make more money in less time. Before the end of every day, you should fill in the daily organizer for the following day. And before the end of each week, you should fill in the weekly organizer for the next week. The monthly and yearly organizers are less important for day-to-day affairs and you will refer to them primarily when making long-term plans. Under the "Urgent" column of the daily organizer, list the tasks that are most important and make sure that they get done. Then, if you get distracted with unforeseen tasks and can't finish all of your plans for the day, at least you will have done the most important.

If you do not prioritize your tasks you will tend to give first priority to those tasks that come to mind and that are the most time sensitive. Often these are not the most important tasks for increasing the profitability of your business.

Organizers are also important for listing appointments and events. By using your organizers for listing appointments, events, and tasks, you will get into the habit of referring to them frequently and will increase your efficiency at work.

The *staffing calendar* will be quite valuable even if you have only two or three employees. By planning staff assignments on the same piece of paper, you can easily reassign work among different people. For example, by filling in the staffing calendar you might see that two employees are planning to do the same task—allowing you to simply change assignments.

By using the staffing calendar and organizers, you will also be able to project more accurately when you will complete projects and when you will be able to start new ones: your customers will particularly appreciate this.

While all of the forms in this chapter are useful, The

Daily Organizer is an extremely powerful personal management tool that creates more time in every working day. Once you start using the daily organizer you'll wonder how you ever got by without it!

12- OR 24-WEEK PROJECT PLANNER

Project name: _____

Start date: _____

Phase/Description	Duty	1	2	3	4	5	6	7	8	9	10	11	12

Phase/Description	Duty	13	14	15	16	17	18	19	20	21	22	23	24

DAILY ORGANIZER

Date: _____

Time		Urgent
6:00		
:30		
7:00		
:30		
8:00		
:30		
9:00		
:30		
10:00		
:30		
11:00		
:30		
12:00		
:30		
1:00		
:30		
2:00		
:30		
3:00		
:30		
4:00		
:30		
5:00		
:30		
6:00		
:30		
7:00		
:30		
8:00		
:30		
9:00		
:30		
10:00		

Path on CD-ROM: Time Planners (09)→Daily Organizer.xls

MEETING PLANNER

Date: _____

Time	Subject	Persons Attending	Urgent
6-6:30			
6:30-7			
7-7:30			
7:30-8			
8-8:30			
8:30-9			
9-9:30			
9:30-10			
10-10:30			
10:30-11			
11-11:30			
11:30-12			
12-12:30			
12:30-1			
1-1:30			
1:30-2			
2-2:30			
2:30-3			
3-3:30			
3:30-4			
4-4:30			
4:30-5			
5-5:30			
5:30-6			
6-6:30			
6:30-7			
7-7:30			
7:30-8			
8-8:30			
8:30-9			
9-9:30			
9:30-10			
10-10:30			

MONTHLY ORGANIZER

Month of: _____

	Morning	Afternoon	Evening
1			
2			
3			
4			
5			
6			
7			
8			
9			
10			
11			
12			
13			
14			
15			
16			
17			
18			
19			
20			
21			
22			
23			
24			
25			
26			
27			
28			
29			
30			
31			

Comments: _____

NOTES

Date: _____

PROJECT TIME SHEET

Name: _____

Department: _____

For week of: _____

Project name	Project number	Mon.	Tues.	Wed.	Thur.	Fri.	Total hours per project
							0
							0
							0
							0
							0
							0
							0
							0
							0
							0
							0
							0
							0
							0
							0
							0
							0
							0
							0
							0
							0
							0
							0
							0
							0
							0
							0
							0
							0
							0
							0
							0
							0

Path on CD-ROM: Time Planners (09)→Project Time Sheet.xls

REMINDER

Date: _____

Things to Do

1		
2		
3		
4		
5		
6		
7		
8		
9		
10		
11		
12		
13		
14		
15		
16		
17		
18		
19		
20		
21		
22		
23		
24		
25		

Follow-Up

1		
2		
3		
4		
5		
6		
7		

Path on CD-ROM: Time Planners (09)→Reminder.xls

STAFFING CALENDAR

Date from: _____

Date to: _____

Employee	Monday	Tuesday	Wednesday	Thursday	Friday	Saturday	Sunday

Path on CD-ROM: Time Planners (09)→Staffing Calendar.xls

WEEKLY ORGANIZER

Week beginning: _____

Ending: _____

Time	Monday	Tuesday	Wednesday	Thursday	Friday	Saturday	Sunday
6:00							
:30							
7:00							
:30							
8:00							
:30							
9:00							
:30							
10:00							
:30							
11:00							
:30							
12:00							
:30							
1:00							
:30							
2:00							
:30							
3:00							
:30							
4:00							
:30							
5:00							
:30							
6:00							
:30							
7:00							
:30							
8:00							
:30							
9:00							
:30							
10:00							
:30							
11:00							

Path on CD-ROM: Time Planners (09)→Weekly Organizer.xls

YEARLY ORGANIZER-1

For year: _____

	January	February	March	April	May	June
1						
2						
3						
4						
5						
6						
7						
8						
9						
10						
11						
12						
13						
14						
15						
16						
17						
18						
19						
20						
21						
22						
23						
24						
25						
26						
27						
28						
29						
30						
31						

YEARLY ORGANIZER-2

For year: _____

	July	August	September	October	November	December
1						
2						
3						
4						
5						
6						
7						
8						
9						
10						
11						
12						
13						
14						
15						
16						
17						
18						
19						
20						
21						
22						
23						
24						
25						
26						
27						
28						
29						
30						
31						

Path on CD-ROM: Time Planners (09)→Yearly Organizer-2.xls

Time Savers

Chapter 10

Forms that speed office communication

It bears repeating—time is money. The forms in this chapter are designed to make communication within a business as fast, simple, and efficient as possible.

The basic *memo* and *phone memo* forms can save a lot of time. Instead of writing out a long note, an employee can jot down two names, one check mark, and three explanatory words to make a complete memo-type message. Why waste time with intricate office communication when you could be spending time on revenue-producing work with customers?

The *memo/response form* is a variation on the memo that will not only save you time in delivering a message but, more importantly will also speed a reply by telling the person on the other end that they only need to jot down a few words in response—not produce a detailed, elaborate reply.

The *routing label* can save time in two ways. The first is that the label takes about two seconds to fill out. More importantly, a routing label presents a clear instruction for the same item to pass from one person to the next. This avoids copying or reproducing the item or having to personally deliver it to every person on the list.

The *items needed form* can save more time than you think. By having this form in a visible place, anyone can request (but not automatically receive) any supply they feel will improve their work. Having this form readily available means that the person responsible for ordering supplies does not have to be interrupted every time someone needs to order a special-colored pen. It also means that when you do need a supply ordered, you don't have to waste time looking for the person who orders supplies—you can merely add it to the list.

In addition to saving time, forms such as these will add to your business a touch of professionalism which is an essential component of employee morale.

CHECK REQUEST

Date: _____

Needed by: _____

Amount sought: _____

Department/Address: _____

Amount authorized: _____

_____

Explanation: _____

Account number: _____

_____

_____

Check number: _____

_____

_____

Date: _____

_____

Authorized by: _____

Received by: _____

Department/Title: _____

Path on CD-ROM: Time Savers (10)→Check Request.xls

FAX COVER SHEET

Date: _____

Page 1 of _____ pages

To: _____

Company: _____

From: _____

Company: _____

Regarding: _____

Remarks: [ ] Urgent   [ ] For your review   [ ] Reply ASAP   [ ] Please comment

_____

_____

_____

_____

_____

_____

_____

_____

_____

_____

_____

_____

_____

_____

_____

_____

_____

_____

_____

_____

_____

_____

_____

_____

_____

_____

_____

Path on CD-ROM: Time Planners (10)→Fax Cover Sheet.xls

IMPORTANT MESSAGE

For: _____

Date: _____ Time _____ | am | pm |

M _____

of _____

Phone _____

Fax _____

Mobile _____

	Telephoned		Please call
	Came to see you		Will call again
	Wants to see you		Rush
	Returned your call		Will fax you

Message: _____

_____

_____

_____

_____

Signed: _____

IMPORTANT MESSAGE

For: _____

Date: _____ Time _____ | am | pm |

M _____

of _____

Phone _____

Fax _____

Mobile _____

	Telephoned		Please call
	Came to see you		Will call again
	Wants to see you		Rush
	Returned your call		Will fax you

Message: _____

_____

_____

_____

_____

Signed: _____

IMPORTANT MESSAGE

For: _____

Date: _____ Time _____ | am | pm |

M _____

of _____

Phone _____

Fax _____

Mobile _____

	Telephoned		Please call
	Came to see you		Will call again
	Wants to see you		Rush
	Returned your call		Will fax you

Message: _____

_____

_____

_____

_____

Signed: _____

IMPORTANT MESSAGE

For: _____

Date: _____ Time _____ | am | pm |

M _____

of _____

Phone _____

Fax _____

Mobile _____

	Telephoned		Please call
	Came to see you		Will call again
	Wants to see you		Rush
	Returned your call		Will fax you

Message: _____

_____

_____

_____

_____

Signed: _____

Path on CD-ROM: Time Planners (10)→Important Message.xls

INCOMING PHONE LOG

Date	Time	Call for	Call from	Of	Message	Please call	Will call again	Returned your call

Path on CD-ROM: Time Planners (10)→Incoming Phone Log.xls

ITEMS NEEDED

Date submitted: _____
Date needed: _____

Submitted by: _____   Destination: _____

_____   _____

_____

_____   Attention: _____

_____

Item/Description	Quantity	Price per	Price	Date needed
			$ -	
			$ -	
			$ -	
			$ -	
			$ -	
			$ -	
			$ -	
			$ -	
			$ -	
			$ -	
			$ -	
			$ -	
			$ -	
			$ -	
			$ -	
			$ -	
			$ -	
			$ -	

Total Cost $ -

Specifications/Suppliers to contact

_____

_____

_____

MEMO -RESPONSE

From: _____   To: _____

_____   _____

Date: _____   RE: _____

MEMO	RESPONSE

By: _____   _____

_____   _____

MEMO

Date prepared: _____

Subject: _____

From: _____

To: _____

Subject: _____

☐ Urgent   ☐ For Your Information

☐ Respond   ☐ Please Comment

☐ Other

_____

_____

_____

_____

_____

_____

_____

_____

_____

_____

_____

_____

_____

_____

_____

_____

_____

_____

Path on CD-ROM: Time Planners (10)→Memo.xls

OUTGOING PHONE LOG

Date	Length of call	Employee	Department	Person called	Company	City	Area code	Telephone number

Path on CD-ROM: Time Planners (10)→Outgoing Phone Log.xls

PHONE CALL

Date: _____ Time: _____ | am
For: _____ | pm
_____ | Phoned
M _____ | Returned your call
of _____ | Please call
_____ | Will call again
Phone _____ | Came to see you
Message _____ | Wants to see you
_____ | Will fax you
_____ | Rush
Signed _____ |

PHONE CALL

Date: _____ Time: _____ | am
For: _____ | pm
_____ | Phoned
M _____ | Returned your call
of _____ | Please call
_____ | Will call again
Phone _____ | Came to see you
Message _____ | Wants to see you
_____ | Will fax you
_____ | Rush
Signed _____ |

PHONE CALL

Date: _____ Time: _____ | am
For: _____ | pm
_____ | Phoned
M _____ | Returned your call
of _____ | Please call
_____ | Will call again
Phone _____ | Came to see you
Message _____ | Wants to see you
_____ | Will fax you
_____ | Rush
Signed _____ |

Path on CD-ROM: Time Planners (10)→Phone Call.xls

PHONE MEMO

Date: _____

Time: _____ [ ] am   [ ] pm

Call for: _____

Call from: _____

Of company: _____

Phone number: _____

Please call [ ]

Phoned [ ]

Returned your call [ ]

Will call again [ ]

Message: _____

_____

_____

_____

_____

_____

_____

Taken by: _____

ROUTING LABEL

Material ID: _____

Date: _____

Route to: _____

_____

_____

_____

_____

_____

_____

_____

_____

_____

Examine and pass on to next name on list

ROUTING LABEL

Material ID: _____

Date: _____

Route to: _____

_____

_____

_____

_____

_____

_____

_____

_____

_____

Examine and pass on to next name on list

ROUTING LABEL

Material ID: _____

Date: _____

Route to: _____

_____

_____

_____

_____

_____

_____

_____

_____

_____

Examine and pass on to next name on list

ROUTING LABEL

Material ID: _____

Date: _____

Route to: _____

_____

_____

_____

_____

_____

_____

_____

_____

_____

Examine and pass on to next name on list

Path on CD-ROM: Time Planners (10)→Routing Label.xls

Personnel Records

Information required by law

A business with even one employee cannot operate without detailed personnel records. The law requires all employers, no matter how small, to maintain complete and separate records for each employee, including a *W-4 form*, an *employment eligibility verification form*, and thorough records of wages and payroll taxes paid and withheld. Forms provided to help you assemble and summarize this information include: *weekly time sheet; employee time sheet; payroll record; group payroll record; wage report; employee attendance record; quarterly payroll record/deductions*; and *quarterly payroll record/wages*. Stiff penalties can be incurred for not maintaining these records.

With today's increased litigation and unemployment insurance liabilities, employers need to take extreme care in firing employees. One step to reduce the possibility of an unjustified lawsuit is to document a problem employee's performance with such forms as the *employee absentee report* and *the employee warning notice* before firing an employee.

Of course the best way to avoid problem employees is to hire excellent workers in the first place. Our detailed *employment application* can help you evaluate a job candidate carefully before making a hiring decision.

Remember that government agencies have little tolerance for even small employers that do not keep employee records. For example, if a previous employee makes a claim for unemployment insurance, the unemployment office will not even listen to an employer's opinion unless the employer can first promptly provide complete gross wage information, exact hiring date, and exact final work date.

ADVANCE REQUEST

Date: _____

Amount desired: _____   For: _____

Amount authorized: _____   Approved by: _____

Check/Voucher number: _____   Title/Department: _____

Explanation: _____
_____
_____
_____

Signed: _____

Date: _____

Amount desired: _____   For: _____

Amount authorized: _____   Approved by: _____

Check/Voucher number: _____   Title/Department: _____

Explanation: _____
_____
_____
_____

Signed: _____

Path on CD-ROM: Personnel Records (11)→Advance Request.xls

AUTHORIZATION TO RELEASE INFORMATION

From: _____

_____

_____

To: _____

_____

_____

I have applied for a position with: _____

I have been requested to provide information for their use in reviewing my background and qualifications. Therefore, I authorize the investigation of my past and present works, character, education, military and employment qualifications.

The release in any manner of all information by you is authorized whether such information is of record or not, and I do hereby release all persons, agencies, firms, companies, etc., from any damages resulting from providing such information.

This authorization is valid for 90 days from the date of my signature below. Please keep this copy of my release request for your files. Thank you for your cooperation.

Signature: _____   Date: _____

Witness: _____   Date: _____

Medical information is often protected by state laws and civil codes. Consult your attorney if you wish to seek this information.

EMPLOYEE ABSENTEE REPORT

Date: _____

Name: _____

Department: _____

Check Reason	
	Sick
	Vacation
	Permission
	Unknown
	Other

Was absent from work today

Remarks _____
_____
_____
_____
_____
_____
_____
_____
_____
_____

Signature of Supervisor: _____

Official Signature: _____

Path on CD-ROM: Personnel Records (11)→Employee Absentee Report.xls

EMPLOYEE ATTENDANCE RECORD

For Year: _____

Name: _____

Employee Number: _____

Social Security Number: _____

	Jan	Feb	Mar	Apr	May	Jun	Jul	Aug	Sep	Oct	Nov	Dec
1												
2												
3												
4												
5												
6												
7												
8												
9												
10												
11												
12												
13												
14												
15												
16												
17												
18												
19												
20												
21												
22												
23												
24												
25												
26												
27												
28												
29												
30												
31												

Attendance Codes

X = Excused absence   S = Sick   UA = Unexcused absence   V = Vacation   JD = Jury Duty

EMPLOYEE MONTH-BY-MONTH EVALUATION SURVEY

Name: _____

Year: _____

Jan ☐ Excellent ☐ Very Good ☐ Good ☐ Average ☐ Below Average ☐ Needs Improvement
Comments: _____

Feb ☐ Excellent ☐ Very Good ☐ Good ☐ Average ☐ Below Average ☐ Needs Improvement
Comments: _____

Mar ☐ Excellent ☐ Very Good ☐ Good ☐ Average ☐ Below Average ☐ Needs Improvement
Comments: _____

Apr ☐ Excellent ☐ Very Good ☐ Good ☐ Average ☐ Below Average ☐ Needs Improvement
Comments: _____

May ☐ Excellent ☐ Very Good ☐ Good ☐ Average ☐ Below Average ☐ Needs Improvement
Comments: _____

Jun ☐ Excellent ☐ Very Good ☐ Good ☐ Average ☐ Below Average ☐ Needs Improvement
Comments: _____

Jul ☐ Excellent ☐ Very Good ☐ Good ☐ Average ☐ Below Average ☐ Needs Improvement
Comments: _____

Aug ☐ Excellent ☐ Very Good ☐ Good ☐ Average ☐ Below Average ☐ Needs Improvement
Comments: _____

Sep ☐ Excellent ☐ Very Good ☐ Good ☐ Average ☐ Below Average ☐ Needs Improvement
Comments: _____

Oct ☐ Excellent ☐ Very Good ☐ Good ☐ Average ☐ Below Average ☐ Needs Improvement
Comments: _____

Nov ☐ Excellent ☐ Very Good ☐ Good ☐ Average ☐ Below Average ☐ Needs Improvement
Comments: _____

Dec ☐ Excellent ☐ Very Good ☐ Good ☐ Average ☐ Below Average ☐ Needs Improvement
Comments: _____

Path on CD-ROM: Personnel Records (11)→Employee Month-by Month Evaluation.xls

EMPLOYEE REFERENCE CHECK

Applicant: _____

Supervisory duties: _____
_____

Supervisory ability: _____
_____

Leadership potential: _____
_____

Attendance/punctuality: _____
_____

Work with others: _____
_____

Reason for leaving: _____
_____

Would you re-hire: _____
_____

Other comments: _____
_____

References checked: _____

Date: _____

Path on CD-ROM: Personnel Records (11)→Employee Reference Check.xls

EMPLOYEE ROSTER

Name	Address	Phone

Path on CD-ROM: Personnel Records (11)→Employee Roster.xls

EMPLOYEE SEPARATION NOTICE

Date: _____

Name: _____

Department: _____

	Check Reason	Left our employ today
	Lack of Work	Remarks _____
	Sick	_____
	Absence	_____
	Injury	_____
	Death	_____
	Retired	_____
	Quit	_____
	Other	_____
		_____
		_____
		_____

Signature of Supervisor: _____

Official Signature: _____

EMPLOYEE TIME SHEET

From _____   To: _____

Name: _____

Number: _____

Department: _____

Date	Morning		Afternoon		Office Use Only	
	In	Out	In	Out	Regular Hrs	Overtime Hrs

Signature: _____ | 0 | 0 |

Path on CD-ROM: Personnel Records (11)→Employee Time Sheet.xls

EMPLOYEE WARNING NOTICE

☐ 1st notice

☐ 2nd notice

Date: _____

Name: _____

Department: _____

Violation		Remarks:
	Late Arrival	_____
	Early Departure	_____
	Absent	_____
	Attitude	_____
	Safety Violation	_____
	Defective Work	_____
	Other	_____
		_____
		_____
		_____

Signature of Supervisor: _____

Official Signature: _____

Path on CD-ROM: Personnel Records (11)→Employee Warning.xls

EMPLOYMENT APPLICATION PART 1

> Prospective applicants will receive consideration without discrimination because of race, color, religion, sex, national origin, age, marital or veteran status, non-job-related medical conditions or handicaps, or any other legally-protected status.

Date of application: _____

Position(s) applied for: _____

How did you hear about this position?

Advertisement ☐   Friend ☐   Relative ☐   Walk-in ☐

Employment agency ☐   Other ☐

Name: _____
Last   First   Middle

Address: _____
Number   Street   Apt no.

_____
City   State   Zip

Telephone: _____

Social Security No.: _____

Please check response

	Yes	No
If employed and under 18, can you furnish a work permit?	☐	☐
Have you applied for work here before?	☐	☐
If "Yes," give date		
Have you even been employed here before?	☐	☐
If "Yes," give date		
Are you employed now?	☐	☐
May we contact your present employer?	☐	☐
Are you prevented from lawfully becoming employed in this country because of Visa or Immigration Status?	☐	☐

(Prood of citizenship or immigration status will be required upon employment.)

On what date will you be able to work? _____

Please check the category that best summarizes your available hours

☐ Full-time   ☐ Part-time
☐ Shift work ☐ Temporary

	Yes	No
Can you travel if the job requires it?	☐	☐
Are you on a lay-off and subject to recall?	☐	☐
Have you ever been convicted of a felony within the last five years?	☐	☐

If "Yes," please explain _____

_____

	Yes	No
Are you a veteran of the U.S. Military?	☐	☐
If "Yes," specify branch		
Was your discharge other than honorable?	☐	☐

If "Yes," please explain _____

	High School	College/University	Graduate/Professional
School name, location			
Years Completed/Degree			
Diploma/Degree			
Describe course of study			
Outline specialized training, apprenticeships, internships, skills, and extracuricular activities			

Honors Received: State any additional information you feel may be helpful to us in considering your application. If necessary, please use a separate sheet of paper.

_____

_____

_____

List professional, trade, business, or civic activities and offices held.
(You may exclude memberships that would reveal sex, race, religion, national origin, age, ancestry, or handicap or other protected status.)

_____

_____

_____

Please list the name, address, and daytime telehone number of three references who are not related to you and are not previous employers.

_____

_____

_____

Briefly summarize special skills and qualifications you have acquired from your employment or other experience.

_____

_____

_____

Do you speak a foreign language? If so, note below; please list your ability to read and write in that language.

_____

_____

_____

Employment History

Please give an accurate, complete employment record, filling out all sections. Start with your present or last job. Include military service assignments and volunteer activities. You may exclude organization names that may disclose your race, religion, color, national origin, gender, handicap, or other protected status.

Employer Telephone	Dates Employed		Work Performed
	From	To	
Address			
Job Title	Hourly Rate/Salary		
	Starting	Final	
Supervisor			
Reason for leaving			
Employer Telephone	Dates Employed		Work Performed
	From	To	
Address			
Job Title	Hourly Rate/Salary		
	Starting	Final	
Supervisor			
Reason for leaving			
Employer Telephone	Dates Employed		Work Performed
	From	To	
Address			
Job Title	Hourly Rate/Salary		
	Starting	Final	
Supervisor			
Reason for leaving			

If you need additional space, please continue on a separate sheet of paper.

Signature

The information provided in this Employment Application is true, correct, and complete. If employed, any misstatement or omission of fact on this application may result in my dismissal.

I authorize you to engage a consumer reporting agency to investigate my credit and personal history. If a report is obtained you must provide, at my request, the name and address of the agency so I may obtain from them the nature and substance of the report.

I understand that an offer of employment does not create a contractual obligation upon the employer to continue to employ me in the future.

Date	Signature

GROUP ATTENDANCE RECORD

Date: _____

Name	In	Arrived Late (specify)	Left Early (specify)	Vacation Day	Sick/Personal Day

Path on CD-ROM: Personnel Records (11)→Group Attendance Record.xls

GROUP PAYROLL RECORD

Date from: _____

Date to: _____

Employee	Exemptions	Hours Worked Regular	Hours Worked Overtime	Rate Regular	Rate Overtime	Wages/Salary Regular	Wages/Salary Overtime	Total Wages Paid
						$ -	$ -	$ -
						$ -	$ -	$ -
						$ -	$ -	$ -
						$ -	$ -	$ -
						$ -	$ -	$ -
						$ -	$ -	$ -
						$ -	$ -	$ -
						$ -	$ -	$ -
						$ -	$ -	$ -
						$ -	$ -	$ -
						$ -	$ -	$ -
						$ -	$ -	$ -
						$ -	$ -	$ -
						$ -	$ -	$ -
						$ -	$ -	$ -
						$ -	$ -	$ -
						$ -	$ -	$ -
						$ -	$ -	$ -
						$ -	$ -	$ -
						$ -	$ -	$ -
						$ -	$ -	$ -
						$ -	$ -	$ -
						$ -	$ -	$ -
						$ -	$ -	$ -
						$ -	$ -	$ -
						$ -	$ -	$ -
						$ -	$ -	$ -
						$ -	$ -	$ -
						$ -	$ -	$ -
						$ -	$ -	$ -

Total Wages Paid/Group $ -

GROUP TIME SHEET

Date: _____

Name	Morning		Afternoon		Office Use Only	
	In	Out	In	Out	Regular Hrs	Overtime Hrs
						0	0

Path on CD-ROM: Personnel Records (11)→Group Time Sheet.xls

NEW EMPLOYEE EVALUATION SURVEY

Date: _____

Name: _____

Day 1: ☐ Excellent ☐ Very Good ☐ Good ☐ Average ☐ Below Average ☐ Needs Improvement
Comments: _____
_____

Day 2: ☐ Excellent ☐ Very Good ☐ Good ☐ Average ☐ Below Average ☐ Needs Improvement
Comments: _____
_____

Day 3: ☐ Excellent ☐ Very Good ☐ Good ☐ Average ☐ Below Average ☐ Needs Improvement
Comments: _____
_____

Day 4: ☐ Excellent ☐ Very Good ☐ Good ☐ Average ☐ Below Average ☐ Needs Improvement
Comments: _____
_____

Day 5: ☐ Excellent ☐ Very Good ☐ Good ☐ Average ☐ Below Average ☐ Needs Improvement
Comments: _____
_____

Day 6: ☐ Excellent ☐ Very Good ☐ Good ☐ Average ☐ Below Average ☐ Needs Improvement
Comments: _____
_____

Day 7: ☐ Excellent ☐ Very Good ☐ Good ☐ Average ☐ Below Average ☐ Needs Improvement
Comments: _____
_____

Day 8: ☐ Excellent ☐ Very Good ☐ Good ☐ Average ☐ Below Average ☐ Needs Improvement
Comments: _____
_____

Day 9: ☐ Excellent ☐ Very Good ☐ Good ☐ Average ☐ Below Average ☐ Needs Improvement
Comments: _____
_____

Day 10: ☐ Excellent ☐ Very Good ☐ Good ☐ Average ☐ Below Average ☐ Needs Improvement
Comments: _____
_____

PAYROLL RECORD

Person	Hourly Rate	Weekly Rate	Annual Rate

Gross payroll costs	$ -
Employer's share of payroll taxes	
Total Payroll Costs	$ -

INDIVIDUAL PERSONNEL RECORD

Name: _____   Employee #: _____

Address: _____

City: _____   State/Zip: _____

Phone: _____

Dates of Employment

From: _____   To: _____

Date(s) entered in file:

	Application
	Resume
	References

_____

_____

_____

Required Tax Forms

_____

_____

_____

_____

	Attendance Record
	Wage Report
	Advance Request
	Absentee Report
	Warning Notice

_____

_____

_____

_____

_____

Path on CD-ROM: Personnel Records (11)→Personnel Record.xls

PRE-EMPLOYMENT REFERENCE CHECK

From: _____   Date: _____

_____

_____

To: _____

_____

_____

We would appreciate your assistance in verifying the information listed below regading an employment application. It is to be understood that all information is confidential and will be treated as such in our company personnel files. Attached, please find an authorization to release information signed by the applicant. A self-addressed, stamped envelope is enclosed for your convenience in replying. We appreciate your assistance in this matter. Thank you.

Yours truly,

_____

Personnel Manager

The following information was provided to us by the applicant. Please make any appropriate corrections:

Name: _____   SS#: _____

Job title: _____   Final salary: _____

Date of employment: _____

Reason for termination _____

Please complete the following information:

Would you re-hire this applicant?   ☐ Yes   ☐ No

If no, why not? _____

Please review and rate the applicant in these areas:

	Unsatisfactory			Average				Outstanding	
Attendance	☐ 1		☐ 2		☐ 3		☐ 4		☐ 5
Quality of work	☐ 1		☐ 2		☐ 3		☐ 4		☐ 5
Quantity of work	☐ 1		☐ 2		☐ 3		☐ 4		☐ 5
Cooperation	☐ 1		☐ 2		☐ 3		☐ 4		☐ 5
Responsibility	☐ 1		☐ 2		☐ 3		☐ 4		☐ 5

Signed _____

Title: _____   Date: _____

PRE-EMPLOYMENT REFERENCE CHECK LETTER

Applicant: _____   Position: _____

Company contacted: _____   Phone: _____

Name of company representative: _____

Title of company representative: _____

Dates of employment: _____

Salary information:

Regular pay: _____   Overtime pay: _____

Bonus _____   Shift differential: _____

Date of last wage increase: _____

What was your relationship with the applicant? _____

_____

What were the applicant's job title and duties? _____

_____

_____

How long did you supervise this employee? _____

How would you compare this employee to others doing similar work and responsibilities? _____

_____

_____

Strong points: _____

_____

_____

_____

_____

Areas for improvement: _____

_____

_____

_____

_____

How would you rate this applicant's ability on a scale of 1 to 5 (5 being the highest) regarding the following:

Attention to detail: _____   Comment: _____

Learn: _____   Comment: _____

Follow directions: _____   Comment: _____

Accept responsibility: _____   Comment: _____

Follow through: _____   Comment: _____

Initiate: _____   Comment: _____

Path on CD-ROM: Personnel Records (11)→Pre-Employment Reference Check Letter.xls

QUARTERLY PAYROLL RECORD / DEDUCTIONS

Employee name: _____

Employee number: _____

Quarter number

1	2	3	4

Check Number	Net Pay	Deductions						
		Insurance	Withholding Taxes					Social Security
				Local	State	Federal		
	$ -	$ -	$ -	$ -	$ -	$ -		$ -
	$ -	$ -	$ -	$ -	$ -	$ -		$ -

QUARTERLY PAYROLL RECORD / WAGES

Employee name: _____

Employee number: _____

Quarter Number

1	3
2	4

Week Ending	Hours								Rate		Wages		Total Wages
	S	M	T	W	T	F	S	Regular / Overtime	Regular	Overtime	Regular	Overtime	
											$ -	$ -	$ -
											$ -	$ -	$ -
											$ -	$ -	$ -
											$ -	$ -	$ -
											$ -	$ -	$ -
											$ -	$ -	$ -
											$ -	$ -	$ -
											$ -	$ -	$ -
											$ -	$ -	$ -
											$ -	$ -	$ -
											$ -	$ -	$ -
											$ -	$ -	$ -
											$ -	$ -	$ -
											$ -	$ -	$ -
											$ -	$ -	$ -
											$ -	$ -	$ -

Quarterly Totals: 0   0 $ - $ - $ -

VACATION REQUEST

Date: _____

Name: _____

Department: _____

Dates:

From: _____

To: _____

	Total vacation days accrued
	Total vacation days taken
	Total vacation days available
	Number of days requested
	Total vacation days remaining (if request approved)

Approval: _____

Manager Signature: _____

Date: _____

WAGE REPORT

Period from: _____

Period to: _____

Employee: _____

Social Security number: _____

INCOME

	Number of Hours	Rate	Total
Regular Hours			$ -
Overtime Hours			$ -
Vacation			$ -
			$ -
			$ -

Gross Earnings $ -

DEDUCTIONS

Social Security (FICA): _____

Federal withholding tax: _____

State withholding tax: _____

Local withholding tax: _____

Other: _____

Total Deductions: $ -

Net Wages: $ -

Path on CD-ROM: Personnel Records (11)→Wage Report.xls

WEEKLY TIME SHEET

From: _____   To: _____

Name: _____

Number _____

Department: _____

		Morning		Afternoon		Office Use Only	
		In	Out	In	Out	Regular Hrs	Overtime Hrs
Monday							
Tuesday							
Wednesday							
Thursday							
Friday							
Saturday							
Sunday							

Total Hours | 0 | 0 |

Signature: _____

Results
Trackers

Chapter 12

Forms that evaluate your performance

The forms in this section are essential for preparing a tax return and are also vital for evaluating the performance and well-being of your business.

Your income tax forms will be very similar to the *profit and loss statement*. If your business is incorporated, you will also need to submit a beginning-and end-of-year balance sheet similar to the *corporate balance sheet form*.

While the profit and loss statement is an important gauge of the success and health of a business, the *balance sheet* is generally a better indicator. For example, a business might show a huge profit on the profit and loss statement—but if the profit is tied up in bad debt and excess inventory then the business might be experiencing cash flow difficulty which could lead to bankruptcy. That is why banks and other lenders place particular importance on balance sheets. You should too. Keep a careful eye to see if receivable and inventories are growing faster than sales.

If your business is not incorporated, banks will want to see the *individual/partnership balance sheet*. If the balance sheet for your partnership reflects only business assets, the bank will also want to see personal balance sheets from all partners. If your business is incorporated but somewhat smaller than General Motors, the bank will want to see a personal balance sheet in addition to the corporate balance sheet and will almost certainly ask you to personally guarantee any loans.

Trade creditors will often ask for a copy of your balance sheet but, unlike the bank, seldom ask for a copy of your Income Statement.

The *profit and loss variance form* helps you pinpoint areas in which you may be able to cut costs by showing you the difference from one year (or month) to the next.

The *straight line depreciation form* helps you calculate depreciation for tax purposes and for creating your balance sheet.

While the number of forms in this section is not large, these forms are fundamental business tools that you should refer to frequently. In fact, in many instances you will benefit by assembling and examining a profit and loss statement or a balance sheet every month!

BALANCE SHEET

Company Name: _____

Balance Sheet as of: _____

ASSETS   LIABILITIES

Cash		Accounts payable	
Marketable securities		Sales tax payable	
Accounts receivable		Payroll payable	
Inventory		Payroll taxes payable	
Prepaid expenses		Income taxes payable	
		Accruals	
Total current assets	$ -	Total current liabilities	$ -
Land		Notes payable	
Buildings			
Equipment			
Accumulated depreciation			
Leasehold improvements			
Amortization of L.H. imp.			
Total fixed assets	$ -	Total long-term liabilities	$ -
Deposits		Draws	
Long-term investments		Paid in capital	
Deferred assets		Retained earnings prior	
		Retained earnings current	
Total long-term assets	$ -	Total equity	$ -
Total Assets	$ -	Total Equity and Liabilities	$ -

Note: Total Assets must equal Total Equity and Liabilities

CORPORATE BALANCE SHEET

ASSETS

Cash:	
Accounts Receivable:	
Inventory:	
Loan to stockholders:	
Depreciable, depletable and intangible assets:	
Other assets:	
Less accumulated depreciations, depletion and amortization:	
Less bad debt allowance:	

Total Assets:	$ -

LIABILITIES

Accounts payable:	
Taxes:	
Other current liabilities:	
Loans from stockholders:	
Mortgages, notes, bonds payable:	
Other liabilities:	
Capital stock:	
Paid-in or capital surplus:	
Retained earnings:	
Less cost of treasury stock:	

Total Liabilities and Stockholder's Equity:	$ -

INDIVIDUAL/PARTNERSHIP BALANCE SHEET

ASSETS

Cash:	
Accounts receivable:	
Inventory:	
Loan to partners, key employees:	
Depreciable, depletable and intangible assets:	
Real estate:	
Other assets:	
Less accumulated depreciations, depletion and amortization:	
Less bad debt allowance:	
Total Assets:	$ -

LIABILITIES

Accounts payable:	
Taxes:	
Other current liabilities:	
Loans:	
Mortgages, notes, bonds payable:	
Other liabilities:	
Net worth:	
Total Liabilities:	$ -

PROFIT AND LOSS STATEMENT

Year: _____

INCOME

Gross sales:	
Less returns:	
Less bad debts:	
Interest, rent, royalty income:	

Total Income:	$ -

EXPENSES

Cost of goods sold:	
Direct payroll:	
Indirect payroll:	
Taxes, other than income tax:	
Sales expenses:	
Shipping, postage:	
Advertising, promotion:	
Office expenses:	
Travel, entertainment:	
Phone:	
Other utilities:	
Auto/truck:	
Insurance:	
Professional fees:	
Rent:	
Interest on loans:	
Other:	

Total Expenses before Tax:	$ -
Total Income:	$ -
Net Income:	$ -
Income Tax:	

Net Income after Tax:	$ -

PROFIT & LOSS VARIANCE

Year _____

or Month: _____

	Previous Year	Estimate	Actual	Difference	Percent Difference
Gross sales:				$ -	
Less returns:				$ -	
Less bad debt:				$ -	
Interest, rent, royalty income:				$ -	
				$ -	
Total Income:	$ -	$ -	$ -	$ -	

EXPENSES

	Previous Year	Estimate	Actual	Difference	Percent Difference
Cost of goods sold:				$ -	
Direct payroll:				$ -	
Indirect payroll:				$ -	
Taxes, other than income tax:				$ -	
Sales expenses:				$ -	
Shipping, postage:				$ -	
Advertising, promotion:				$ -	
Office expenses:				$ -	
Travel, entertainment:				$ -	
Phone:				$ -	
Other utilities:				$ -	
Auto/truck:				$ -	
Insurance:				$ -	
Professional fees:				$ -	
Rent:				$ -	
Interest on loans:				$ -	
Other:				$ -	

	Previous Year	Estimate	Actual	Difference	Percent Difference
Total Expenses before Tax:	$ -	$ -	$ -	$ -	
Total Income:	$ -	$ -	$ -	$ -	
Net Income:	$ -	$ -	$ -	$ -	
Income Tax:				$ -	
Net Income after Tax:	$ -	$ -	$ -	$ -	

Path on CD-ROM: Results Trackers (12)→Profit & Loss Variance.xls

RATIO ANALYSIS

For month ending: _____

Current Ratio = Current Assets ÷ Current Liabilities
Current Ratio = _____ ÷ _____ = _____ This Year
Current Ratio = _____ ÷ _____ = _____ Last Year

Inventory Turnover = Cost of Goods Sold ÷ Inventory
Inventory Turnover = _____ ÷ _____ = _____ This Year
Inventory Turnover = _____ ÷ _____ = _____ Last Year

Total Asset Turnover = Net Sales ÷ Total Assets
Total Asset Turnover = _____ ÷ _____ = _____ This Year
Total Asset Turnover = _____ ÷ _____ = _____ Last Year

Average Collection Period = Accounts Receivable ÷ Average Credit Sales/Day
Average Collection Period = _____ ÷ _____ = _____ This Year
Average Collection Period = _____ ÷ _____ = _____ Last Year

Long-Term Debt to Equity = Long-Term Debt ÷ Stockholders Equity
Long-Term Debt to Equity = _____ ÷ _____ = _____ This Year
Long-Term Debt to Equity = _____ ÷ _____ = _____ Last Year

Total Debt to Total Assets = Total Liabilities ÷ Total Assets
Total Debt to Total Assets = _____ ÷ _____ = _____ This Year
Total Debt to Total Assets = _____ ÷ _____ = _____ Last Year

Long-Term Debt to Equity = Long-Term Debt ÷ Total Equity
Long-Term Debt to Equity = _____ ÷ _____ = _____ This Year
Long-Term Debt to Equity = _____ ÷ _____ = _____ Last Year

Path on CD-ROM: Results Trackers (12)→Ratio Analysis.xls

STRAIGHT-LINE DEPRECIATION SCHEDULE

Item/Description	Date placed in service	Total cost paid	Depreciation recovery in yrs	Total depreciation	Annual depreciation	Depreciation Time	
						From	To

Total Depreciation $ -

Prepared by: _____

Date: _____

Path on CD-ROM: Results Trackers (12)→Straight-Line Depreciation Schedule.xls

Business Growers

Chapter 13

Forms that plan the future

By planning your business future carefully you can increase your profits, build confidence with your banker, and foresee any cash flow problems long before they occur.

It is extremely important in the *pro forma profit and loss projection* to assume differing levels of sales. It is impossible to ever project sales precisely, but it is usually possible to project sales fairly accurately within a range. Then, assuming different sales levels, you should plan to adjust your expenses accordingly to maintain the best possible profit margin. In making a presentation to a bank, you will want to show at least three different assumptions for levels of sales.

Interestingly, the very time that your business experiences strong sales and fast growth is the time it can very likely run out of cash and credit. This is because receivables and inventory will normally increase even faster than sales. So, if you are planning for your business to grow quickly (and who isn't?) you need to plan your future cash needs very carefully.

The *pro forma cash flow* will help you project your receipt of cash and your disbursement of cash to determine net cash needs. Be sure to project receipt of invoices realistically for vendors of your size in your industry, which will probably be after your stated terms. Remember as you establish credit with your vendors that you will be able to stretch out payments to the industry standard time.

The *five-year balance sheet* will also be useful for planning cash flow for the future. Key variables are accounts receivable, cash, and inventory. Although your bank might be willing to meet your initial seasonal accounts receivable financing needs, they might not be willing to increase the financing as quickly as you are planning to increase your accounts receivable.

FIVE-YEAR BALANCE SHEET PLANNER

ASSETS

Cash:					
Accounts receivable:					
Inventory:					
Loan to stockholders:					
Depreciable, depletable, and intangible assets:					
Other assets:					
Less accumulated depreciation, depletion, and amortization:					
Less bad debt allowance:					
Total Assets:	$ -	$ -	$ -	$ -	$ -

LIABILITIES

Accounts payable:					
Taxes:					
Other current liabilities:					
Loans from stockholders:					
Mortgages, notes, bonds payable:					
Other liabilities:					
Capital stock:					
Paid-in or capital surplus:					
Retained earnings:					
Less cost of treasury stock:					
Total Liabilities and Stockholder's Equity:	$ -	$ -	$ -	$ -	$ -

Path on CD-ROM: Business Growers (13)→5-Year Balance Sheet Planner.xls

FIVE-YEAR PRO-FORMA CASH FLOW

	Year #1	Year #2	Year #3	Year #4	Year #5
INFLOW					
Cash on hand beginning of month:					
From sales:					
From interest, etc.:					
Loan proceeds:					
Inflow plus cash on hand:	$ -	$ -	$ -	$ -	$ -
OUTFLOW					
Cost of goods sold:					
Direct payroll:					
Indirect payroll:					
Taxes, other than income tax:					
Sales expenses:					
Shipping, postage:					
Advertising, promotion:					
Office expenses:					
Travel, entertainment:					
Phone:					
Other utilities:					
Auto/truck:					
Insurance:					
Professional fees:					
Rent:					
Interest on loans:					
Taxes:					
Loan pay-down::					
Other:					
Cash outflow subtotal:	$ -	$ -	$ -	$ -	$ -
Net cash on hand, end of year:	$ -	$ -	$ -	$ -	$ -

BUSINESS START-UP CASH NEEDS

Basic one-time costs

Real estate deposit:	
Phone deposit:	
Other utility deposit:	
Rent before opening:	
Phone before opening:	
Other utilities before opening:	
Payroll before opening:	
Remodeling costs:	
Equipment costs:	
Fixtures, furniture, signs:	
Legal fees:	
Accounting fees:	
Subtotal:	$ -

Starting inventory/raw goods

Detail: _____

Subtotal:	$ -

Initial advertising/promotion

Detail: _____

Subtotal:	$ -

Reserve for _____

Detail: _____

Subtotal:	$ -

Total:	$ -

PRO-FORMA CASH FLOW

Year _____

	Jan	Feb	Mar	Apr	May	Jun	Jul	Aug	Sep	Oct	Nov	Dec
INFLOW												
Cash on hand EOM:												
From sales:												
From interest, etc.:												
Loan proceeds:												
Inflow plus cash on hand:	-	-	-	-	-	-	-	-	-	-	-	-
OUTFLOW												
Cost of goods sold:												
Direct payroll:												
Indirect payroll:												
Taxes, other than income tax:												
Sales expenses:												
Shipping, postage:												
Advertising, promotion:												
Office expenses:												
Travel, entertainment:												
Phone:												
Other utilities:												
Auto/truck:												
Insurance:												
Professional fees:												
Rent:												
Interest on loans:												
Taxes:												
Loan pay-down:												
Other:												
Cash outflow subtotal:	-	-	-	-	-	-	-	-	-	-	-	-
Net cash on hand EOM:	-	-	-	-	-	-	-	-	-	-	-	-

PRO-FORMA PAYROLL RECORD

Person	Hourly Rate	Weekly Rate	Annual Rate

Gross payroll costs	$ -
Employer's share of payroll taxes	
Total Payroll Costs	$ -

PRO-FORMA PROFIT & LOSS

Year: _____

or Month: _____

	Previous Year	Sales Scenarios		
		Weak	Likely	Good
Gross sales:				
Less returns:				
Less bad debt:				
Interest, rent, royalty income:				
Total Income:	0	0	0	0

EXPENSES

Cost of goods sold:				
Direct payroll:				
Indirect payroll:				
Taxes, other than income tax:				
Sales expenses:				
Shipping, postage:				
Advertising, promotion:				
Office expenses:				
Travel, entertainment:				
Phone:				
Other utilities:				
Auto/truck:				
Insurance:				
Professional fees:				
Rent:				
Interest on loans:				
Other:				

Total Expenses before Tax:	0	0	0	0
Total Income:	0	0	0	0
Net Income:	0	0	0	0
Income Tax:				
Net Income after Tax:	0	0	0	0

Assumptions and Comments on Financial Statements

This page contains critical set-up questions and assumptions that should be filled out before
any of the financial spreadsheets are begun.

Assumptions:	Enter here:	Instruction:
Name of Plan:	My Business Plan	What is the Name of the plan to be used in the page headers on financial reports?
Starting Month:	1	What is the Starting Month of the plan? (Range 1-12)
Starting Year:	1999	What is the Starting Year of the plan? (Range 1-5)
Years:	5	What is the Number of Years to be covered by the plan? (Range 1-5)
Commissions %:	5.00	What percentage of Sales will Commissions be? (range 0-100) (Enter "0" if not applicable or highly variable.)
Freight Costs %:	0.00	What percentage of sales will Freight costs run? (Range 0-100)
Payroll Tax Rate:	13.00	What percentage of gross payroll will the Employer's Share of Payroll Taxes plus the cost of employee benefits run? (Range 0-100)
Income Tax Rate:	35.00	What percentage of net income do you estimate all Income Taxes (city, state, federal) will run? (Range 0-100)
Days Inventory:	0	How many Days of Invetory (in other words how many days of sales it would take to exaust the inventory if it were not replenished) will you stock? (Range 0 to 1080). (If your business will not have inventory enter "0").
Cost of Sales %:	50.00	What percentage of sales will Cost of Sales be? Enter 0 if you will not have Cost of Sales. (Range 0-100)
Credit Sales?:	N	Will you make any Sales On Credit? (Y/N)
Credit Sales %:	100.00	What percentage of your sales will be for credit (Range 0-100)
Days Credit:	30	How many days will credit customers take on average to pay you back? (Range 0-90)
Cost of Sales A/P?:	N	Will you Buy Inventory or any other items or materials that you sell or provide to customers (and will be listed costs of sale of your profit and loss statement) On credit? (Y/N)
Cost of Sales A/P %:	100.00	What percentage of direct cost items will be bought on credit? (Range 0-100)
Cost of Sales Days A/P:	30	Enter the number of days that you will take to pay for direct cost items bought on credit? (Range 0-90)
General:	N	Other than inventory, will you buy any other Expense Items On Credit? (Y/N)
General A/P %:	100.00	What percentage of non payroll-related (and non-inventory) expense items will you buy on credit? (Range 0-100)
Days General A/P:	30	How many days will you take to pay for non payroll-related (and non-inventory) expense items that you buy on credit? (Range 0-90)
S-T Interest Rate:	10.00	What do you estimate your annual interest rate will be for short-term debt? (Range 0-100) (Enter "0" if you will not have short-term debt.)
L-T Interest Rate:	11.00	What do you estimate your annual interest rate will be for long-term debt? (Range 0-100) (Enter "0" if you will not have long-term debt.)

STARTING BALANCE SHEET

Assets	Balance

Current Assets

Cash	$
Accounts Receivable	$
Inventory	$
Other Current Assets	$
Total Current Assets	$

Long Term Assets

Depreciable Assets	$
Net Depreciable Assets	$
Non-Depreciable Assets	$
Total Long Term Assets	$

Total Assets	$

Liabilities & Equity

Current Liabilities

Current Liabilities	$
Cost of Sales A/p	$
Non-Cost of Sales A/P	$
Short-Term Debt	$
Income Taxes Due	$
Total Current Liabilities	$

Long Term Debt	$

Equity

Stock &Paid-in Capital	$
Retained Earnings	$
Total Equity	$

Total Liabilities & Equity	$

Note: Total Assets must equal
        Total Liabilities & Equity

Marketing & Sales
    Commissions
    Literature & Mailings
    Advertising & Publicity
    Other Marketing
General & Admin.
    Payroll
    Payroll Taxes, Benefits
    Facilities & Equip Rent
    Maintenance & Repairs
    Utilities, Phone, Postage
    Insurance
    Supplies
    Freight
    Auto Travel & Entertain
    Legal & Accounting
    Other Outside Services
    Misc. Taxes, Fees
    Depreciation
    Other G&A Expenses
Non-Operating Costs
    Interest

Below this point you may enter any additional assumptions and comments you wish to have appear printed in the business plan about the finacial projections:

Enter any additional assumptions or comments you would like to make in the following space:

_____
_____
_____
_____
_____
_____
_____
_____
_____
_____
_____
_____
_____
_____

Developed by Adams Media, **BusinessTown.com** is a free informational site for entrepreneurs, small business owners, and operators. It provides a comprehensive guide for planning, starting, growing, and managing a small business.

Visitors may access hundreds of articles addressing dozens of business topics, participate in forums, as well as connect to additional resources around the Web. **BusinessTown.com** is easily navigated and provides assistance to small businesses and start-ups. The material covers beginning basic issues as well as the more advanced topics.

✓ **Accounting**
Basic, Credit & Collections, Projections, Purchasing/Cost Control

✓ **Advertising**
Magazine, Newspaper, Radio, Television, Yellow Pages

✓ **Business Opportunities**
Ideas for New Businesses, Business for Sale, Franchises

✓ **Business Plans**
Creating Plans & Business Strategies

✓ **Finance**
Getting Money, Money Problem Solutions

✓ **Letters & Forms**
Looking Professional, Sample Letters & Forms

✓ **Getting Started**
Incorporating, Choosing a Legal Structure

✓ **Hiring & Firing**
Finding the Right People, Legal Issues

✓ **Home Business**
Home Business Ideas, Getting Started

✓ **Internet**
Getting Online, Put Your Catalog on the Web

✓ **Legal Issues**
Contracts, Copyrights, Patents, Trademarks

✓ **Managing a Small Business**
Growth, Boosting Profits, Mistakes to Avoid, Competing with the Giants

✓ **Managing People**
Communications, Compensation, Motivation, Reviews, Problem Employees

✓ **Marketing**
Direct Mail, Marketing Plans, Strategies, Publicity, Trade Shows

✓ **Office Setup**
Leasing, Equipment, Supplies

✓ **Presentations**
Know Your Audience, Good Impression

✓ **Sales**
Face to Face, Independent Reps, Telemarketing

✓ **Selling a Business**
Finding Buyers, Setting a Price, Legal Issues

✓ **Taxes**
Employee, Income, Sales, Property, Use

✓ **Time Management**
Can You Really Manage Time?

✓ **Travel & Maps**
Making Business Travel Fun

✓ **Valuing a Business**
Simple Valuation Guidelines

Instructions for CD-ROM

Adams Streetwise Business Forms

Adams Streetwise Business Forms was designed to serve as a comprehensive business resource, providing you with the forms you need to run your business in the real world.

These forms will help you to manage your finances, close sales, track employee performance, and much, much more. Compatible with all major word processors, this program enables you to quickly develop forms to use as a standard across your organization.

If you want to find one of the forms from the book on the enclosed CD-ROM, simply insert the disk, click on Open a Master Document and follow the steps outlined at the bottom of the form you have chosen.

SYSTEM REQUIREMENTS
Minimum Requirements
486 PC compatible or higher
Windows 95/98 or NT
2X CD-ROM
8MB of RAM
5MB of free hard drive space

Recommended
486 PC compatible or higher
Windows 95/98 or NT
6X CD-ROM or faster
16MB of RAM or more
20MB of free hard drive space

Installation
Windows 95, 98, & NT

Place disk in CD-ROM drive and close the drive door. Most CD-ROMs will auto-run the installation after the drive door closes. If your CD-ROM does not auto-run, follow the simple procedures below.

1) From the Start Menu choose Run.
2) When the Run Window appears, **click** on the Browse button on your right.
3) From the drop down menu, select your CD-ROM drive.
4) Double-click on the file titled "Setup."
5) When the Run Window reappears, Click the Ok button.

By accepting the defaults, the program should install successfully.

TROUBLE SHOOTING

ALWAYS BE SURE THE CD IS IN THE DRIVE

Note that these forms contain a large amount of information in comparison to most items that you print. Occasionally, this may cause a print buffer error on some printers.

To fix, try following these steps.

1) Go to your My Computer icon and double-click.
2) Double-click on the Printer icon.
3) Highlight the printer you are using and go under the File menu and choose Properties.
4) Click on the Details Tab.
5) Hit the button for Spool Settings.
6) Write down you current setting for spool data format.
7) Check off Print directly to Printer.
8) Close all the dialog boxes you have opened and re-start our program.

If you try printing now, it should work, though it may be slow.

To restore your former printer settings, follow the steps above, but choose Spool printer jobs so printing finishes faster and restore your spool data format to what you wrote down above.

The procedure above should fix this problem on most printers. If not please contact technical support.

NOTE:
Updating your printer drivers may also correct your problem. Most major manufacturers have their drivers available for download directly from their website.

How to Reach Us
By Mail: Adams Media Corporation
          260 Center Street
          Holbrook, MA 02343
By phone: (781) 767-4128
By Fax: (781) 767-2055
By email: support@adamsmedia.com

Technical Support hours are Monday through Friday, between 9 AM and 5 PM, Eastern Time. Before calling, please make sure your computer is turned on, with Adams Streetwise program running and on the screen. When you reach an Adams Media technical support specialist, be prepared to give the following information:

1) The version of Adams Streetwise program (Located in the Help>About section of the program)
2) The type of computer you are using (486, Pentium, model, etc.)
3) The operating system software you are using (Windows 95, 98, Windows NT)

Please note that, when technical support is extremely busy, you may reach voice mail. We have implemented this system to insure you are not paying long distance charges while you are on hold. Please leave a message and someone will get back to you within one business day.